The So[...] Book Of Fine Old Recipes

by

Lillie S. Lustig
S. Claire Sondheim
Sarah Rensel

APPLEWOOD BOOKS
Bedford, Massachusetts

The Southern Cook Book Of Fine Old Recipes

was originally published in

1935

ISBN: 978-1-4290-1125-9

Thank you for purchasing an Applewood book.
Applewood reprints America's lively classics—
books from the past that are still of interest
to the modern reader.
For a free copy of
a catalog of our
bestselling
books,
write
to us at:
Applewood Books
Box 365
Bedford, MA 01730
or visit us on the web at:
For cookbooks: foodsville.com
For our complete catalog: awb.com

Prepared for publishing by HP

THE SOUTHERN COOK BOOK

OF FINE OLD RECIPES

Compiled and
Edited by

Lillie S. Lustig
S. Claire Sondheim
Sarah Rensel

Decorations by

H. Charles Kellum

Copyrighted 1935

CULINARY ARTS PRESS

P. O. Box 915, Reading, Pa.

INDEX

■

INDEX

'Case Cookin's lak religion is—
Some's 'lected an' some ain't,
An' rules don' no mo' mek a cook
Den sermons mek a saint.

From "BANDANNA BALLADS"

By HOWARD WEEDEN

INDEX

∎

Introduction

•

PEOPLE think of the Southland as the place where the sun shines brighter, the breezes are gentler, the birds sing sweeter and the flowers are fairer. We, who have edited this cook book, which we hope you will find helpful, think of the Southland as the hearthstone of superb cooking. To attempt a Southern Cook Book in one small pamphlet was an ambitious undertaking. There were many fine recipes that should have been included but lack of space would not permit. It became the editors' problem to select as many, as varied and as useful a collection of recipes as it was possible to include in these few pages. Many fine dishes had to be omitted to make way for better ones.

The natural, geographic and climatic advantages of the different sections of the sunny South have played an important part in Dixie cookery. The fertile fields, plentiful fruit trees and waterways have each contributed bountifully. Every part of the Southland is individual and distinctive in its cookery. The "Creole Dish" of New Orleans has nothing to do with racial origin but rather indicates the use of red and green peppers, onions and garlic. Oranges, grapefruit and avocados play an important part in Florida cookery. Maryland is famous for its fried chicken and its delicious sea food recipes. One thinks of Virginia, its hot breads and its sugar-cured hams. Kentucky is known for its corn "likker" and its flannel cakes. Only one thing is universally true: Every corner of the South is famous for its fine cookery.

As you glance through this book you will find many delicious dishes . . . many excellent combinations. You will find here the carefully-guarded secrets of real Southern cooking, palatable and tempting to the eye. You will find accurate, tried and tested recipes . . . each one a gastronomical delight.

The very name "Southern Cookery" seems to conjure up the vision of the old mammy, head tied with a red bandanna, a jovial, stoutish, wholesome personage . . . a wizard in the art of creating savory, appetizing dishes from plain everyday ingredients. But it should be remembered that not all the good cooks of the Southland were colored mammies . . . or folks who lived on plantations. Southern city folks are also famous for their hospitality, their flare for entertaining and the magnificence of their palate-tickling culinary efforts. Most of the recipes in this book were gathered from this latter source, though they undoubtedly in many cases owe their origin to the colored mammies who rarely bothered to write down their recipes . . . for they were good cooks who most often could neither read nor write . . . didn't have to . . . you just put 'em in front of a stove with the fixin's and they created somethin' grand . . . even if they couldn't always 'splain you jus' how.

All your life you have heard of the traditionally famous dishes of the Southland. No names appear so frequently on hotel menus as Dixie names. No cooking seems more famous or synonymous with quality and deliciousness than Southern cooking. You will find here, published for the first time in book form, we believe, the truly amazing recipe for "Kentucky Burgoo", and the celebrated recipe for "Pot Likker", which is a familiar dish in almost every part of the South, particularly in the homes of the poor white and the negro. We believe this book to contain a remarkable cross-section of fine recipes and we hope you will find it a valuable aid in your culinary efforts.

I layed m' head on de railroad track.
Thought about m' yaller gal, and took it back.
Oh honey, how long?

KENTUCKY BURGOO

(This recipe makes 1200 gallons)

"Kentucky Burgoo" is the celebrated stew which is served in Kentucky on Derby Day, at Political Rallies, Horse Sales and at other outdoor events. This recipe is from a handwritten copy by Mr. J. T. Looney, of Lexington. Mr. Looney is Kentucky's most famous Burgoo-maker and it was for him that Mr. E. R. Bradley named his Kentucky Derby winner "Burgoo King". Mr. Looney uses a sauce of his own in the preparation of this truly-amazing concoction.

Mr. Looney is invited to all parts of the country to prepare Burgoo for large gatherings. This is not a dish to be attempted by an amateur though it can be prepared in smaller quantities. It is a very picturesque sight to see Mr. Looney, aided by many negro assistants, preparing this dish over open fires and huge kettles which are kept simmering all night.

  600 pounds lean soup meat (no fat, no bones)
  200 pounds fat hens
2000 pounds potatoes, peeled and diced
  200 pounds onions
    5 bushels of cabbage, chopped
   60 ten-pound cans of tomatoes
   24 ten-pound cans puree of tomatoes
   24 ten-pound cans of carrots
   18 ten-pound cans of corn
      Red pepper and salt to taste
      Season with Worcestershire, Tabasco, or A#1 Sauce

Mix the ingredients, a little at a time, and cook outdoors in huge iron kettles over wood fires from 15 to 20 hours. Use squirrels in season . . . one dozen squirrels to each 100 gallons. (See Recipe Page 13.)

"Burgoo is literally a soup composed of many vegetables and meats delectably fused together in an enormous caldron, over which, at the exact moment, a rabbit's foot at the end of a yarn string is properly waved by a colored preacher, whose salary has been paid to date. These are the good omens by which the burgoo is fortified."

                     —*"Carey's Dictionary of Double Derivations"*

POT LIKKER

(Made famous by the late Senator Huey P. Long)

Into 3 quarts of cold water, put a ½-pound piece of salt pork and place on fire to boil for 45 minutes. Wash young turnip greens in several waters and clean them well. Put them into the pot along with the pork and let boil for another hour. Drain the water from the greens and meat; chop the greens rather fine and season well with salt and pepper. Place the greens on a hot dish and on top arrange slices of the pork; pour over the greens and meat about 1½ cups of the water in which the greens were cooked (pot likker). Cornmeal dodgers are frequently served along with this dish and are arranged around the greens.

CORN MEAL DODGER FOR POT LIKKER

  ½ pint white corn meal
  ½ teaspoon salt
   2 tablespoons melted butter or other shortening
      cold water

Add salt to corn meal and stir in the melted butter. Add sufficient cold water so dough will hold shape. Mould dough into biscuit size pieces and drop into boiling pot likker. Cook in closely covered pot for twenty minutes. Serve garnished with the greens from the "pot likker".

Kentucky, oh Kentucky,
  How I love your classic shades,
Where flit the fairy figures
  Of the star-eyed Southern maids;
Where the butterflies are joying
  'Mid the blossoms newly born;
Where the corn is full of kernels,
  And The Colonels Full of Corn!

                  Will Lampton.

Chicken Gumbo

1 small stewing chicken
2 tablespoons flour
3 tablespoons butter, melted
1 onion, chopped
4 cups okra, sliced and chopped
2 cups tomato pulp
few sprigs parsley, chopped
4 cups water
salt and pepper to taste

After chicken is cleaned and dressed, cut it into serving portions. Dredge lightly with the flour and sauté in the butter, along with the chopped onion. When the chicken is nicely browned, add the okra, tomatoes, parsley and water. Season to taste with salt and pepper. Cook very slowly until the chicken is tender and the okra well-cooked—about 2½ hours. Add water as required during the slow cooking process. If a thin soup is preferred, the quantity of water may be increased.

Almond Chicken Soup

½ cup blanched almonds
6 bitter almonds
3 cups chicken broth
1 teaspoon onion juice
1 bay leaf, crushed fine
3 tablespoons butter
3 tablespoons flour
2 cups milk
1 cup cream
salt and pepper to taste

Chop almonds fine, adding the bitter almonds for a more pronounced flavor. Add the chopped almonds to the chicken broth, seasoned with onion juice and bay leaf. Simmer slowly. Melt the butter and stir in the flour; when smooth, add to the broth, stirring constantly until the boiling point is reached. Add the milk and cream and season to taste with salt and pepper.

Southern Bean Soup

1 cup dried beans
cold water
6 cups ham broth
1 cup chopped celery
½ onion, minced
3 tablespoons butter
3 tablespoons flour
salt and pepper

Cover the beans with cold water and let stand overnight, or at least six hours. Drain off water and add beans to ham broth. Add the celery and onion and let cook slowly until beans become quite soft. Strain the bean broth; press the beans through a sieve and add the pulp to the strained broth. If necessary, add more water in order to have five cups of broth. Melt the butter, stir in the flour, salt and pepper; slowly stir in the hot bean broth and simmer until thickened. Serve hot with slices of lemon and hard cooked eggs.

Some folks say preachers won't steal,
But I caught two in my cornfield.
One had a bushel, one had a peck,
One had a roastin' ear hung round his neck.

Chicken Cream Soup

3 cups chicken broth
3 tablespoons rice
½ cup diced celery
2 cups hot milk

Cook the rice and celery until soft. Strain and rub through a strainer and add to the stock. Add 2 cups of hot milk, season with salt and pepper to taste. Sprinkle chopped parsley over the top when ready to serve.

Okra Soup

1 soup bone
4 cups cold water
4 cups okra, cut fine
2 cups tomato pulp
salt and pepper

Cover soup bone with cold water and allow to come to a boil; cook about one hour. Add the okra which has been cut fine and the tomato pulp. Simmer all together for 2 hours until thick. Rice is invariably served with this soup and sometimes corn and buttered beans.

Black Bean Soup

2 cups black beans
12 cups water
¼ pound salt pork
½ pound lean beef, cut in small pieces
1 carrot, diced
3 small onions, minced
3 cloves
¼ teaspoon mace
dash red pepper
3 hard cooked eggs, sliced
1 lemon, sliced
1 wineglass sherry

Wash and clean beans and soak over night. In the morning, sort carefully and add to the water with the salt pork, the lean beef, the carrot, onion and seasonings. Cover and cook slowly for 3 hours, or until beans have become very soft. Rub through a sieve, place in a tureen; add the sliced eggs, the lemon and the glass of sherry.

Southern Gumbo

2 tablespoons butter, melted
1 onion, chopped
2 cups tomatoes
2 cups okra, cut fine
1 cup chopped green peppers
2 cups hot water
½ teaspoon celery seed
salt and pepper

Fry the onions in the melted butter until brown; add the vegetables, hot water and seasonings. Cook slowly until quite thick.

Maryland Cream of Crab Soup

1 tablespoon flour
2 tablespoons butter
2 quarts milk
1 pint crab meat
½ onion sliced
½ pint heavy cream
chopped parsley, celery, salt, pepper

Melt butter in top of double boiler, add flour and blend. Gradually add the milk and onion, parsley and celery, and season to taste. Cook slowly until the soup thickens a little, then add the crab meat. Serve in individual dishes with a spoonful of whipped cream on top.

Crab Soup, Baltimore

2 tablespoons butter
1 onion, finely chopped
1 tablespoon flour
2 cups warm water
1 cup crab meat
¼ cup chopped celery
chopped parsley
salt and pepper
dash Tabasco sauce
3 cups scalded milk

Melt the butter, add the onion and brown. Blend in the flour and slowly add the warm water; allow to cook until slightly thickened. Add the crab meat, celery, parsley and seasonings. Allow to simmer for 30 minutes. Just before serving, add the scalded milk.

Oyster Soup

1 quart oysters
1 quart rich milk
2 tablespoons butter
1 tablespoon finely-chopped parsley
dash onion salt or 1 teaspoon onion juice
salt and pepper to taste

Strain the oysters, put oyster broth in a saucepan. Into a double boiler pour the milk. Heat the oyster broth but do not boil. When both are hot add the broth to the milk, stir. Add the butter and seasoning, then gradually one by one put the oysters in and heat until hot but never let it boil. When the oysters puff and the edges crinkle, serve at once.

Shrimp Gumbo

2 quarts fresh shrimp
3 onions
½ cup vinegar
salt
2 quarts water
1 tablespoon butter, melted
1 tablespoon flour
4 cups okra, cut fine
1 cup cooked rice
6 large tomatoes, skinned
2 bay leaves
pinch sugar and pepper

Wash and clean the shrimp. Boil the shrimp with 2 of the onions, the vinegar and salt in the water about 20 minutes. Drain off the stock and save. Shell the shrimp. Chop the remaining onion and brown in the melted butter. Stir in the flour and slowly add the strained broth, stirring constantly. Add the okra and rice, tomatoes, seasonings and shelled shrimp. Let simmer a short time before serving in order to cook okra and tomatoes.

Oyster Bisque

1 quart oysters
1 quart milk
1 tablespoon flour
1 tablespoon butter
½ cup chopped celery
1 green pepper
Worcestershire sauce
salt and pepper

Put oysters through a meat grinder, make a cream soup with milk, thickened with flour and seasoned with butter, salt, pepper, chopped celery and green pepper. Add the oysters and keep the soup hot but do not allow it to boil as it may curdle. Add Worcestershire sauce just before serving.

Chicken Oyster Gumbo

1 small chicken
1 pound of beef cut up for stewing
1 cup diced okra
1 tablespoon butter
1 onion
3 pints water
2 dozen oysters
1½ teaspoons sassafras leaves
salt and pepper

Cut up the chicken and stew it with the beef and 1 cup okra in 3 pints of water. When a strong broth has been obtained and the meat is tender, remove the chicken bones and cut the meat into small pieces. Add the oysters with their liquor and season to taste with salt, pepper and onion browned in butter. Add the sassafras leaves. Cook until the edges of the oysters curl.

Cindy went to meetin'
    She shouted and she squeeled;
She got so much religion
    She broke her stockin' heel.

Creole Soup 'a la Madame Begue

1 tablespoon butter, melted
1 tablespoon chopped green pepper
1 tablespoon chopped red pepper
1 tablespoon flour
1½ cups soup stock
1 cup tomato pulp
½ cup corn
  salt and pepper

Lightly brown the peppers in the melted butter; blend in the flour. Slowly add the soup stock and tomato pulp; place over fire and continue to stir until soup boils. Reduce the heat, cover and let cook slowly for 20 minutes. Strain into another pot, add the corn and season to taste with salt and pepper.

Onion Soup Au Gratin

2 quarts meat broth
8 medium sized onions
2 tablespoons butter
1 teaspoon Worcestershire sauce
  salt and pepper
  toast
  grated parmesan cheese

Slice onions thin and brown in butter. Add the broth, Worcestershire sauce, salt and pepper to taste, and simmer until the onions are tender. Pour soup into an earthen jar or oven-glass casserole. Arrange toast on top of soup, sprinkle with grated cheese and place under the broiler until cheese melts and browns.

Southern Jugged Soup

6 potatoes, sliced
1 onion, sliced
6 tomatoes or two cups canned tomatoes
1 turnip, diced
1 can peas
1 grated carrot
¼ cup rice
3 quarts water
1 tablespoon salt
1 tablespoon sugar
½ teaspoon pepper
1 pinch allspice

Arrange vegetables, rice and seasonings in alternate layers in the bottom of a stone crock with a cover. Boil any carcasses of cold chicken, bones of roast meat or steak with trimmings, in three quarts of water, until the liquid is reduced to two quarts. Strain, cool and remove. Pour the broth over the vegetables. Put on the cover and seal, using tape or muslin, to keep in the steam. Set crock in a pan of hot water. Place in oven and cook from four to six hours.

Plantation Soup

1 carrot, diced
1 stalk celery, cut fine
1 small onion, chopped fine
2 cups soup stock
4 tablespoons butter
2 tablespoons flour
2 cups milk
⅓ cup grated cheese

Cook carrot, celery and onion in the stock until very tender; strain; make a thin white sauce by melting the butter, stirring in the flour and slowly adding the milk. Combine the stock with the white sauce and simmer until blended. When ready to serve, add the grated cheese.

Jellied Mélange

2 tablespoons gelatin
¼ cup cold water
4 cups hot chicken broth
2 tablespoons onion juice
1 cup chopped cooked chicken
½ cup chopped cooked ham
½ cup chopped celery
1 pimiento, chopped fine

Soak the gelatin in the cold water for five minutes. Add to the hot chicken broth with the onion juice and stir until it dissolves. Set aside to cool; when it begins to congeal, stir in the other ingredients, and put in small molds. Chill. Serve on lettuce garnished with mayonnaise and parsley.

Vegetable Bouillon
(General Lee's Favorite Soup)

4 cups tomatoes
1 stalk celery, chopped
2 carrots, chopped
2 sprigs parsley
¼ green pepper, chopped
1 bay leaf
2 teaspoons onion juice
  salt and pepper to taste
1 wineglass sherry wine
2 cups water

Put the tomatoes in a saucepan with the water, add all the vegetables and seasoning and let boil for 30 minutes. Strain. Add the sherry wine. Serve piping hot.

Carry dat load on your head

De Lord will bless your good corn bread.

Ribs of Beef à la Mission

Season short ribs with salt and pepper, also rub over slightly with clove of garlic. Cover with boiling water, add 1 large sliced onion. Cook slowly two hours. Add 2 cups tomatoes, one teaspoon paprika, and cook gently 1 hour.

Veal Paprika

Cut veal steak ½ inch thick. Season with salt and pepper, roll in flour. Heat fat in spider, add paprika until red, then two onions, sliced. Fry slightly, add meat, brown all over, add gradually ½ cup thick sour cream. Cover pan, let cook slowly ½ hour, add a little water and serve.

Old Dominion Veal Fricassee

Cut in pieces 2 pounds veal (loin). Cook slowly in boiling water to cover, add 1 onion, 2 stalks celery, 6 slices carrot. Remove meat. Season with salt and pepper, dredge with flour and brown in butter. Serve with brown sauce.

Calvert Manor Frogs' Legs
(A Dish for the Epicure)

8 frog legs
  boiling salt water
½ cup lemon juice
  salt and pepper
1 egg, beaten
  cracker crumbs

Only the hind legs of the frogs are eaten. Skin the legs and scald them in boiling salt water and lemon juice for about two minutes. Dry after scalding. Season with salt and pepper; dip in beaten egg and then in cracker crumbs. Fry for three minutes in deep fat and serve two frog legs per person.

Parsnips and Salt Pork

2 pounds salt pork
6 parsnips

Cut salt pork in small pieces and partly cover with water and cook until almost done. Then add the parsnips, which have been cut in one-inch pieces. Cook until both the salt pork and parsnips are tender.

Stuffed Pork Chops

Select as many rib pork chops as needed. Have the butcher cut them an inch in thickness and make a pocket in each one. Fill with the following bread filling.

2 cups bread crumbs
1 tablespoon chopped onion
1 cup chopped apples
  season to taste
  hot water to moisten

Place in a baking dish, add a little water to keep from sticking and bake in a slow oven until pork is very well cooked.

Belgian Hare à la Maryland

1 rabbit, cut in portions
  salt and pepper
1 cup flour
2 eggs, beaten
  cracker crumbs
4 tablespoons butter, melted
1 small onion, minced
1 bay leaf
  hot water

Wash pieces of rabbit and wipe well. Sprinkle with salt and pepper and roll each piece in flour, beaten eggs and cracker crumbs. Put in roaster in which the butter was melted, add onion and bay leaf; cover. Roast for 1¼ hours in a moderate oven (350° to 375° F.); baste with hot water, using from 1 to 2 cups depending on amount of gravy desired. Continue to roast, basting frequently, for ½ hour.

Sweetbreads and Mushrooms

1 pair sweetbreads
2 tablespoons butter, melted
2 tablespoons flour
  salt and pepper
2 cups milk
1 pound fresh mushrooms

Parboil sweetbreads and remove all the loose membranes. Sauté in 1 tablespoon of the butter. Blend in 1 tablespoon of the flour; add salt and pepper to taste and 1 cup of milk. Simmer slowly until thickened. Wash and peel the mushrooms, sauté in the remaining butter, blend in the remaining flour, and add the salt and pepper and milk. When thickened, combine with the sweetbread mixture and put in a casserole. Cover with bread crumbs and dot with butter. Brown in a hot oven (400° F.) for 5 to 8 minutes.

Liver à la Madame Begue

1 pound calves' liver, cut in 1-inch cubes
2 small onions, thinly sliced
2 sprigs parsley
  salt and pepper

Sprinkle the liver with salt and pepper, cover with onion and parsley; let stand for 2 hours. Fry in deep fat (390° F.) 1 minute. Drain, garnish with lemon and parsley.

Ah got corn, squash and yams!
Ah got chicken, squirrel, sugar cured hams!

Mock Terrapin Stew

Boil two chickens until tender, cut the meat from the bones and dice it. Beat the yolks of six eggs and set aside. Blend two tablespoons of flour with ¼ pound of melted butter and add one pint of milk heated to the boiling point. Add the beaten yolks, season with salt and pepper. Put back on fire, adding the diced chicken and one large glass of wine just before serving.

Rice and Chicken Casserole

2 cups rice
2 cups milk
1½ tablespoons butter
2 eggs
1 cooked chicken

Bone the chicken and cut into one-inch pieces. Boil the rice in salted water until tender. Stir in the butter, the milk and the eggs. Put a layer of this into a casserole, then the chicken, then the rice. Bake in a (350° F.) moderate oven until well browned.

Dixie Chicken Shortcake

1 large chicken, cooked
2 cups chicken stock
2 tablespoons flour
1 pound mushrooms, cleaned
2 tablespoons butter, melted
  salt and pepper
1 pan cornbread (see page 31)

Remove the skin and bones from the cooked chicken. Cut meat into small pieces. Make a sauce, using 2 cups of the chicken stock and thickening it with the flour. Sauté the mushrooms in the butter. Add the chicken and mushrooms to the sauce. Cut the cornbread into 4-inch squares and split. Cover the lower halves with some of the chicken mixture. Lay on these the top crusts and cover with more of the chicken mixture. Leftover chicken and gravy may also be used in this manner.

Pigeon Pie

4 squabs, parboiled
  rich pastry (see page 37)
3 tablespoons butter, melted
3 tablespoons flour
2 cups stock in which squabs were boiled
1 cup milk
  salt and pepper
  buttered bread crumbs

Fry the parboiled squabs until they are well-browned. Line a deep casserole with rich pastry dough and place the fried squabs in the casserole. Blend 3 tablespoons of flour with the melted butter and slowly stir into the stock and milk. Season with salt and pepper and heat until thickened. Pour the sauce over the squabs; sprinkle buttered bread crumbs on top and place in a hot oven (450° F.) for 10 minutes. Reduce the heat to moderate (350° to 375° F.) and continue baking for 8 to 10 minutes, until crumbs and edges of crust are nicely browned.

I went to the ribber but I didn't go to stay,
But I got so drunk I couldn't get away,
My marster axed we whar I'd been,
And the way he hit me was a sin.

Roast Squab with Rice Pilau

(From the Home of Gentle Folk)

4 squabs
6 slices bacon
1 onion
¾ cup chopped celery
2 cups rice
4 cups chicken stock
4 eggs
  salt and pepper
  mustard pickle juice

Dress the squabs as usual, cleaning them thoroughly. Stuff with a mixture made as follows: Dice bacon and fry until crisp. Remove the bacon, and brown the chopped celery and onions in the bacon drippings. Boil the rice in the chicken stock until tender, then add the bacon, celery and onion. Beat the eggs and add them to the rice. Season with salt and pepper. Stuff the squabs with the mixture and make mounds of the remaining filling on which to lay the squab. Bake in a hot oven for about 25 minutes, basting the squabs frequently with mustard pickle juice.

Chicken à la Tartare

1 broiling chicken
¼ pound melted butter
4 sprigs parsley
1 small onion
¼ pound mushrooms
1 clove of garlic
  salt and pepper
  bread crumbs

Clean the broiler and split it in half. Place it in a frying pan in which the butter has been melted. Chop the parsley, onion, mushrooms and garlic and add to the butter with salt and pepper. Cover the frying pan and allow the broiler to simmer for fifteen minutes, turning it occasionally so that the flavor is absorbed. The chicken is then dipped in bread crumbs and broiled until well browned. The chicken meat is delicately flavored with the mushrooms, onion, garlic, and parsley combination. The pre-cooking in the butter sauce also assures the tenderness of the meat.

Roast Chicken or Turkey

Dredge a four-pound seasoned chicken with flour and place on its back in dripping pan with butter or chicken fat the size of an egg. Place in hot oven (400° F.) and when the flour is browned reduce the heat to (350° F.) moderately hot, then add ¼ cup of fat dissolved in ½ cup boiling water and baste every quarter of an hour. Turn chicken often until breast meat is tender, then it is done. About 1½ hours are required. Turkey will require more liquid and will have to be roasted longer according to size.

Chicken Cakes

1 cup cooked chicken meat, chopped
2 eggs, slightly beaten
1 tablespoon cream
    salt and pepper
    bread crumbs, rolled fine
1 cup White Sauce (see page 24)
½ cup finely chopped celery

Add 1 egg, cream, salt and pepper to the chopped chicken. Make into small flat cakes, dip in the remaining egg mixed with a little milk if desired, and roll in the bread crumbs. Fry on both sides until well browned. Add celery to the white sauce and pour over cakes when ready to serve. Serve on toast and garnish with parsley.

Stewed Chicken and Dumplings

1 chicken
1 cup flour
2 teaspoons baking powder
    milk to make a thick batter
    salt and pepper to taste
    sprig parsley
1 small diced onion

Clean and cut up chicken, place in kettle and partly cover with water, add the chopped onion, salt and pepper and cook until tender. Mix the flour, baking powder, salt and minced parsley and milk to a thick batter and drop from the end of a spoon into the slowly boiling chicken broth, cover tightly and let cook for 20 minutes without raising the lid. Place the chicken on a platter and surround with the dumplings.

Creamed Gravy for Fried Chicken

Take 2 tablespoonfuls of fat from the pan in which you fried the chicken from the recipe for "Fried Chicken Maryland". Add a tablespoon of flour and a cup of thin cream; bring to boiling point, stirring constantly.

Way down yonder on Eagle Creek,
Niggers don't g r o w but eleben feet;
When they're out it ain't no use
To build a ten-foot chicken roost.

*

Barbecued Chicken

1 young broiling chicken
5 tablespoons melted butter
2 tablespoons vinegar
½ teaspoon dry mustard
½ teaspoon Worcestershire sauce
1 pinch red pepper

Split young chickens for broiling. Place them on a broiling rack, skin face down, and cook under moderate flame until well browned and almost tender. Turn and brown the other side. While chicken is cooking, baste frequently with the above mixture.

Fried Chicken Maryland

Select carefully a young tender fryer. Singe and cut into halves or quarters. Wash carefully and dry, then dip into flour to which has been added salt and pepper. Place large piece of butter or chicken fat in an iron skillet and when hot, drop in pieces of chicken and brown quickly on all sides. Reduce heat, add one cup of water and let simmer slowly until done. Remove lid and let chicken fry down slowly. Serve with creamed gravy.

Miss Cecelia's Chicken Pot Pie

1 young chicken
    Pie dough (see page 37)
¼ cup butter
    Salt and pepper
1 cup milk
¼ cup chicken stock

Dress and cut a young chicken weighing 1½ pounds as for frying. Place pieces into a stewpan and barely cover with boiling water. Cook slowly until the meat is tender.

Make pie dough, but use a little less shortening than called for in the recipe. Divide the dough into two parts. Roll out one piece very thin, line the sides of a baking dish with part of it, put in a layer of chicken, and dot with butter, salt and pepper. Cut the rest of this piece of dough into strips, cover the chicken, alternating until all the chicken and dough are used. Add the milk and about ¼ cup of the stock in which the chicken was cooked.

Roll out the second piece of dough, dot with butter, fold and roll again until the butter is blended into the dough. Roll out thin, cover the top of the pie; press the edges together and make small slashes in the crust to allow the steam to escape. Bake the pie in a moderately hot oven (400° F.) until contents are cooked and the crust is well-browned.

Chicken pie is usually served in the same dish in which it was baked.

Chicken Hash

"A Southern Sunday Breakfast Dish—A Northern Luncheon Delicacy"

2 tablespoons butter
1½ tablespoons flour
1 cup chicken stock
2 cups chopped chicken

Make a white sauce with the flour and butter, using the chicken broth in place of milk. When thick, stir in chicken. Place in a buttered casserole and bake. Garnish with slices of toast.

Burgoo For Small Parties

Meat from any domestic beasts or barnyard fowls may be used, along with any garden vegetables desired. Originally, the burgoo was made from wild things found in the woods of Kentucky.

Cut meat to be used into inch cubes; do not throw away bones; add them to meat cubes. Add any dried vegetables which will enhance flavor of stew. Put all materials into large stewing kettle, unless beans and potatoes are being used. If this is the case, cook meats first, and add beans and potatoes about an hour before serving.

Fill kettle half full of water and place over fire to come to a boil. Prepare other vegetables for stew. Peel and halve onions, scrape and dice carrots, pare and cube potatoes. When liquid in kettle is boiling, add vegetables. Lower heat and continue to simmer stew until vegetables are tender. Add salt and seasonings when stew is almost cooked. There should always be enough water to cover the vegetables. Canned tomatoes will add to the flavor of the broth. In a real burgoo, no thickening like meal or rice is used, because the broth is to be strained and served clear. Likewise, sweet vegetables were not used in the real burgoos. (See Page 6.)

Creole Goulash

2 cans red kidney beans
½ pound sliced bacon
1 quart can tomatoes
1 teaspoon baking powder
¼ pound cheese
  salt and pepper

Cook the bacon crisply, then lift it from the pan. Add the kidney beans to bacon fat. Then tomatoes to which baking powder has been added. Stir all together. Season to taste with salt and pepper, put in casserole. Cover closely, set in moderate oven and cook slowly for 1 hour. Then remove the cover and sprinkle with grated cheese, arrange the bacon strips over all and cook for 10 minutes longer. Serve in the casserole.

Corned Beef Hash

"Let No Man Ever Sneer at Hash, Again"

2 tablespoons butter
3 cups cubed boiled potatoes
¾ cup cream
3 teaspoons finely-chopped parsley
2 cups cooked corned beef

Melt the butter in a double boiler, add the potatoes, mix, then pour in the cream, now add the chopped corned beef and the chopped parsley. Stir well but do not mash the potatoes. Place in pan or individual moulds, butter the top and bake until well browned. If desired the top may be indented for raw egg per portion which is dusted with paprika, and baked until egg is set. Garnish with a sprig of parsley.

Jambalayah (a Creole Dish)

1½ cups cold chicken, veal or mutton
1 cup boiled rice
2 large stalks celery
½ green pepper
1 large onion
1½ cups stewed tomatoes
  salt and pepper
  buttered crumbs

Mix together the chicken, rice and tomatoes, and allow them to cook for ten minutes. Then chop and add the onion, green pepper and celery. Turn the mixture into a baking dish and cover with buttered crumbs. Bake for one hour in a moderate oven (350° F.). Serve very hot. This is an excellent way of utilizing left-over meat or chicken.

Aunt Linda's Creole Beef Stew

1½ pounds lean beef
2 cups tomatoes
1 large onion
1 green pepper
1 cup string beans
3 ears or 1 can corn
2 carrots, sliced
  flour, Worcestershire sauce and potatoes as indicated

Place 1½ pounds of lean beef in a casserole or deep iron skillet. Around the beef place as many potatoes as needed, tomatoes, onion, green pepper, string beans, corn, carrots. Sprinkle well with salt and pepper, partially cover with water and place in a slow oven to cook until the meat is done. More water may be added to prevent meat from drying out too much. Remove from pan and place on serving platter and garnish with the vegetables. Add flour to thicken the meat juices and make gravy, using chopped parsley and Worcestershire sauce for the final flavoring.

Roast Duck

("Never Believed Anything Could Taste So Good")

Prepare and clean duck as you would any fowl; rub with salt and pepper. Take 2 tablespoons of ground ginger and rub on both the inside and outside. Peel one onion and into this stick 4 cloves and place on the duck. Place in a roaster and add 1 cup of water. Roast, basting often. Add water when necessary. Stuff duck with bread, apple or mushroom stuffing. The gravy should be highly seasoned and a tart jelly may be added at the last. Serve with baked oranges (see page 26).

Going to the race track
To see my pony run;
If I win any money
Gonna give Cal'donia some.

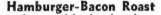

Baked Sliced Ham and Apples

2 large, thin slices raw ham
1 teaspoon dry mustard
2 teaspoons vinegar
½ cup brown sugar
1 tablespoon butter
2 apples

Remove the bone from the ham. Mix together the mustard and vinegar. Spread the mixture thinly on the ham. Slice apples very thin and spread 2 layers on the ham. Sprinkle well with the brown sugar. Roll the ham the long way. Hold together with metal skewers or tie with string. Place in baking pan and dot with butter. Bake in moderate oven for 25 to 30 minutes. Baste several times while baking.

Broiled Hamburger Steak

1 pound chopped beef
2 teaspoons chopped onion
salt and pepper to taste
1 tablespoon cold water
1 tablespoon chopped fat

Mix all together and shape into small round cakes. Place a piece of butter on top of each cake and broil fast on both sides. One pound of beef will make 4 cakes.

Baked Ham

1 slice ham, one inch in thickness
½ cup brown sugar
1 teaspoon dry mustard
2 cups milk

Place ham in baking dish, rub mustard over the top, sprinkle with brown sugar and cover with milk. Bake in a slow oven (300° F.) for one hour.

Broiled Ham

1 slice ham
1 cup milk
1 cup water

Trim all skin from ham and soak in the water and milk for about one hour. Wipe well and place on broiler rack and put under slow flame. Broil slowly and when cooked and slightly browned remove from rack and place on hot platter.

Hamburger-Bacon Roast

3 pounds ground beef and pork
2 large potatoes, cooked and mashed
1 onion, chopped fine
2 slices bread, diced
  chopped parsley
  salt and pepper
3 hard cooked eggs
¼ pound sliced bacon

Combine the meat, potatoes, onion, bread and seasonings. Divide into 2 parts; place one-half in baking pan, cover with the whole hard cooked eggs and the remaining half of the meat. Cover meat with slices of bacon and bake in a moderately hot oven (400° F.) for 1½ hours.

Ham and Pineapple
(Something to Write Home About)

1 slice of ham 1 inch thick, center cut of cured ham
2 cups milk
2 tablespoons butter
1 can sliced pineapple

Soak the ham in the milk for four hours. When ready to cook remove ham from the milk and place in hot pan with the butter. Cook slowly until brown and then turn ham and brown on other side. Transfer ham to another pan and place in warm oven where it will stay hot but not cook. Put slices of pineapple in pan with ham juice and brown on both sides. Then place ham on platter, with slices of browned pineapple on top and around it. Mix the pineapple juice with the ham gravy and pour over the ham.

Smithfield Ham
(The Ham that made Virginia Famous)

Soak ten- to twelve-pound ham for twelve hours, then boil, cooking very slowly for four to five hours, until tender. Cool in its own essence. When cold, remove the skin and make crisscross gashes in the top of the ham with a sharp knife. Sprinkle on top of ham two tablespoons of cracker dust, two tablespoons of brown sugar, and sprinkle lightly with pepper. Stick the ham with whole cloves. A wineglass of sherry sprinkled over the top of the ham will greatly improve the flavor. Bake in a hot oven (450° F.) for twenty minutes until brown. Garnish with watercress and parsley.

Chitterlings
(Chit'lings)

Wash chitterlings thoroughly and cover with boiling salted water. Add 1 tablespoon whole cloves and 1 red pepper cut in pieces. Cook until tender. Drain. Cut in pieces the size of oysters. Dip each piece in beaten egg and then in cracker crumbs. Fry in deep fat until brown. Chitterlings (the smaller intestines of swine) are obtainable at Southern Butcher Shops.

What yuh goin' to do w'en de meat give out?
Goin' to stan' on de cawnah wid mah mouf
*   poked out, mah honey.*

Chicken Terrapin

2 pairs sweetbreads
1 large chicken, cooked
1 quart cream
1 tablespoon cornstarch dissolved in milk
2 egg yolks
1 tablespoon butter
  salt and red pepper
1 wineglass sherry

Parboil the sweetbreads, let cool; remove all the membrane, and cut sweetbreads in small pieces. Cut fine the meat from the chicken which has been cooked and add to the sweetbreads. Place the cream in a double boiler and thicken with the cornstarch which has been dissolved in a little milk. When the cream has been heated thoroughly, add the egg yolks and stir well. Then add the butter and seasoning. When well thickened and hot, stir in the chicken and sweetbreads. Just before serving add one wineglass of sherry. This may be served either on toast or in patty shells.

Roast Partridge

Thoroughly clean four partridges in and outside. Pin over the breast of the partridges a long thin strip of bacon. Rub out and in side with salt and pepper, and put in a roasting pan with a cup of water for 4 partridges. Roast in a hot oven for 30 minutes, basting every 5 minutes. When birds and gravy are a rich brown pour over them a cup of slightly sour cream. Let the cream bubble up in the pan for a minute, baste once more, and serve with gravy poured over the partridges on toast. Garnish with baked oranges.

Louisiana Poultry Sauce

(Sauce Poulette)

1½ cups chicken broth or stock
1 medium onion, sliced
2 tablespoons chopped celery
  salt and pepper
2 egg yolks
2 teaspoons flour
1 tablespoon butter
2 teaspoons tarragon vinegar
2 teaspoons chopped parsley

Place soup stock in saucepan with the onion, celery, salt and pepper and boil four minutes. Mix egg yolks with flour and when well mixed add a tablespoon of cold stock, pour contents of saucepan over the egg mixture very slowly, place on fire again and let thicken, stirring fast and evenly so that the sauce will not curdle. Add butter, vinegar and parsley and stir until butter melts. Strain into gravy dish.

Sometimes I'm up, sometimes I'm down,
Sometimes I'm almost to the groun'!
Altho' you see me going 'long so,
I have my troubles here below!
What makes old Satan hate me so?
'Cause he got me once and let me go!

Crayfish Bisque

2 dozen crayfish
1 quart water
2 onions
2 carrots
2 stalks celery
4 branches parsley
¼ teaspoon thyme
6 tablespoons cracker crumbs
  milk
3 tablespoons butter
2 tablespoons flour
  salt and pepper
1 egg, beaten

Prepare crayfish for soup by soaking in cold water for 30 minutes. Wash carefully; use a brush to remove all the dirt. When cleaned, place in a soup pot with the water, 1 onion, carrots, celery, half the quantity of parsley and the thyme. Allow to come to a boil and continue to cook for 25 minutes. Drain off the water from the crayfish and set aside for later use. Remove all the meat from the heads and bodies of the crayfish; set aside the heads which are to be stuffed. Moisten cracker crumbs with milk. Chop crayfish meat and add to the moistened crumbs. Mince the remaining onion; melt the butter, add the onion and 1 tablespoon of flour. Add 1 tablespoon of the fish broth and the remainder of the parsley. Season with salt and pepper to taste. Simmer slowly for a few minutes; add the crayfish and bread crumb mixture and cook 2 minutes longer. Remove from stove and let cool slightly. Stir in the beaten egg. Fill the crayfish heads with this mixture. Dredge the heads in flour and fry in butter until nicely browned. Drain on paper and keep warm while preparing the stock. Melt the balance of the butter; add the remainder of the flour and stir until smooth. Strain reserved stock in order to remove celery and carrots. Add the broth to the butter and flour. Cook slowly for 12 minutes; season with more salt and pepper if desired. Before serving, add the stuffed crayfish heads.

Planked Shad

3 to 4-pound shad
½ cup melted butter
  salt and pepper
  parsley and lemon

Clean and bone fish. Broil for 10 minutes and then place on a buttered plank, skin side down, season well and pour melted butter over and bake in a hot oven (400° F.) for 15 minutes. Remove from oven and place mounds of mashed potatoes pressed through a pastry bag around the fish. Return to oven until potatoes are brown and fish well done. Garnish with parsley and lemon slices.

Brunswick Stew

2 tablespoons bacon grease
1 frying chicken (about 2 to 2½ pounds)
2 onions
3 cups of water
3 tomatoes, peeled and quartered
½ cup sherry
2 tablespoons butter
½ cup bread crumbs
2 teaspoons Worcestershire sauce
1 pound fresh lima beans
   salt and pepper
½ cup okra
3 ears green corn

Brown the onion in the bacon grease; then add the chicken which has been cut in small pieces and seasoned. When chicken is done, pour off the grease and put chicken and onions in a dutch oven. Add the water, tomatoes, the sherry wine and Worcestershire sauce. Cook slowly over low flame for ½ hour, then add the lima beans, okra and corn cut from the cob. Let simmer one hour. Then add the butter and bread crumbs and cook ½ hour longer.

Barbecued Lamb

   leg of lamb
2 tablespoons Chili sauce
2 onions (sliced)
1 clove garlic
1 tablespoon Worcestershire sauce
1 teaspoon ginger (ground)
1 teaspoon dry mustard
1 tablespoon vinegar
   pepper and salt
2 tablespoons olive oil

After wiping lamb well with a damp cloth rub thoroughly with the spices, which have been mixed together. Dredge well with flour and brown quickly in a hot oven (400° F.) about 25 minutes. Reduce heat and baste with the following sauce made by mixing the Chili sauce, Worcestershire sauce, vinegar and olive oil together. Slice onion and place around the meat with the clove of garlic. Baste every 15 minutes, allowing about 30 minutes to the pound for roasting. One hour before finished add 1 cup of boiling water. Skim fat from pan and strain for gravy.

Barbecue Sauce

¼ pound butter
1 cup vinegar
1 sour pickle, finely chopped
2 tablespoons chopped onion
2 tablespoons Worcestershire sauce
2 tablespoons chili sauce
4 slices lemon
1 teaspoon brown sugar
1 green pepper, finely chopped

Combine all the ingredients and mix thoroughly. Place in a saucepan on a slow fire and cook until butter melts, stirring constantly. Place in top of a double boiler and keep warm until ready to use on barbecued meats or as a sauce for barbecued sandwiches.

Opossum

The opossum is a very fat animal, with a peculiarly flavored meat. It is dressed much as one would dress a suckling pig (for procedure, see recipe below), removing the entrails, and if desired, the head and tail. After it has been dressed, wash thoroughly inside and outside with hot water. Cover with cold water to which has been added 1 cup of salt. Allow to stand overnight; in the morning, drain off the salted water and rinse well with clear, boiling water.

Make a stuffing as follows: Melt 1 tablespoon of butter in a frying pan and add 1 large onion which has been chopped fine. When the onion begins to brown, add the finely chopped liver of the opossum, if desired, and cook until the liver is tender and well done. Add 1 cup of bread crumbs, a little chopped red pepper, a dash of Worcestershire sauce, 1 finely chopped hard cooked egg, salt and water to moisten. Stuff the opossum with the mixture, fastening the opening securely with skewers or by sewing. Put in a roasting pan, add 2 tablespoons of water and roast in a moderate oven (350° F.) until the meat is very tender and richly browned. Baste constantly with the opossum's own fat. When sufficiently roasted, take from the oven, remove the skewers or stitches, and put the opossum on a heated platter. Skim the grease from the gravy remaining in the pan; serve the gravy in a sauceboat. Serve with baked yams or sweet potatoes.

Roast Suckling Pig

For roast suckling pig use only the very young pigs not over six weeks old. Scald them by immersing in very hot water (not boiling) for 1 minute. Remove from the water and use a very dull knife to scrape off hair in order that skin will not be broken. Then cut a slit from the bottom of the throat to the hind legs and remove the entrails and organs, being careful not to break the brains. Wash thoroughly in cold water and chill. Fill with any desired poultry stuffing and sew opening. Roast in a moderate oven (350° F.) from 3 to 4 hours. When serving place a red apple in mouth of pig and serve with candied sweet potatoes and apple sauce.

Apple Ball Sauce for Suckling
(For Goose, Too)

1 cup sugar
1 cup water
4 cloves
   grated rind of ½ lemon
1½ cups apple balls

Make a syrup of the sugar and water, adding the lemon peel and cloves. Cook for several minutes, remove the lemon rind and the cloves and drop in the apples, which have been cut in balls with a potato cutter. Cook until apples are done. Serve with poultry or roasts.

Bouillabaisse

1½ quarts water
1 tablespoon salt
1 pound fresh shrimp
12 cloves
½ pound fresh mushrooms
2 tablespoons butter
2 large onions, chopped
2 buds garlic
2 cups tomato pulp
2 cups water
3 bay leaves
1½ teaspoons curry powder
1 cup grated cheese
½ cup sherry
2 pounds fish fillets (haddock or any boned fish)
1 pound scallops
2 tablespoons flour

Add shrimp, 4 cloves and salt to 1½ quarts of water and bring to a boil. After boiling for 10 minutes remove the shrimp from the pot, saving the broth for later use. Shell the shrimp and cut in half lengthwise. Cut mushrooms into thin slices, add to the shrimp and allow to stand until needed. Melt the butter and fry the onions and garlic in it until golden brown; add the tomato pulp and 2 cups of water, 4 cloves, the bay leaves, curry powder, cheese and ¼ cup of sherry. Allow this mixture to cook slowly for 30 minutes. Season with more salt, if desired. Meanwhile, bring shrimp broth to boiling point, add the fillets of fish, scallops, 4 cloves and ¼ cup of sherry, lower the flame and simmer until fish is sufficiently cooked (about 15 minutes). Combine the shrimp and mushroom mixture with the fish and cook for 5 minutes. Moisten flour with a little cold water and add to the boiling liquid as a slight thickening. Cook another 5 minutes. Remove pieces of fish from the sauce, place on buttered slices of toast on large platter, pour sauce over fish and serve.

Dried Beef à la Maryland

½ pound chipped smoked beef
½ cup thin cream
1 cup milk
1 tablespoon butter
1 scant tablespoon flour
pepper

Soak chipped beef in boiling water for 5 minutes. Drain and dry on a towel. Make a sauce by melting butter in top of double boiler, stir in flour and blend well, then gradually add milk and cream, cook for a few minutes, then add seasonings and beef. Cook 10 minutes and serve on crisp toast.

Chicken Chili Con Carne

1 young chicken
2 tablespoons salt
1 large can tomatoes
3 large onions, chopped
3 buttons of garlic, chopped
1½ teaspoons chili powder
1 quart cooked Mexican beans

Cover the chicken with water and add the can of tomatoes, salt, 2 buttons of garlic and 2 onions. Cook until the chicken is done, remove the chicken from the broth, bone and cut chicken in small pieces and put meat back in the liquid. Heat and while stirring add the chili powder, if more seasoning is desired add more powder. In a separate pan melt 2 tablespoons butter and gently brown the remaining onion and garlic button. Add this to the original mixture and cook for 1 hour. When nearly done add 1 quart of cooked Mexican beans. Cook about 10 minutes longer, just simmering. Serve in deep bowl with crackers.

Pendennis Turtle Soup

(The Soup That Made Kentucky Famous)

2 pounds of veal bones
2 carrots
2 onions
2 tablespoons butter
3 tablespoons flour
2 quarts beef stock or water
1 small can tomatoes
1 small can tomato puree
salt and pepper
whole cloves
½ cup sherry
2 cups boiled fresh turtle meat
1 lemon
2 hard cooked eggs

Roast the bones and vegetables with the butter until brown. Add flour and brown again. Add water or beef stock, tomatoes and tomato puree, salt, black pepper to taste, and a few whole cloves. Boil for two hours. Add sherry wine. Strain the soup through cheesecloth. Then add boiled fresh turtle meat cut in small squares, lemon and eggs, also cut in small squares, boil up quickly and serve.

The Ballad of Bouillabaisse

This Bouillabaisse a noble dish is—
A sort of soup, or broth, or stew,
Or hotchpotch of all sort of fishes,
That Greenwich never could outdo;
Green herbs, red peppers, mussels, saffron,
Soles, onions, garlic, roach, and dace:
All these you eat at Terré's Tavern
In that one dish of Bouillabaisse.

—THACKERAY

Shrimp Sauce

(To Be Served with Fish)

1½ cups chopped cooked shrimps
3 tablespoons lemon juice
  salt and pepper to taste
1½ cups white sauce (see page 24)
2 hard cooked eggs

Soak shrimps in lemon juice one-half hour and add them to white sauce; when ready to serve add the finely chopped hard cooked egg and a little minced parsley. Pour this over the fish.

Deviled Crabs Norfolk

Make a white sauce by mixing one table-spoonful of melted butter and one tablespoon-ful of flour; add one-half cup of cream or milk and let come to a boil, stirring constant-ly. Add salt and pepper. Then add one pint of crab meat, two chopped hard cooked eggs, sprig of parsley, dash of Worcestershire sauce and place in the shells. Brush with melted butter and cracker crumbs and bake in slow oven until well browned.

Crab Croquettes

2 cups crab meat
1 teaspoon onion juice
  salt and pepper
  chopped parsley
1 cup white sauce (see page 24)
  cracker crumbs
1 egg, beaten

Chop the crab meat fine and add the season-ings. When well mixed, add to the white sauce. Mold into croquettes, roll in cracker crumbs, dip in the slightly beaten egg, and then roll in the crumbs again. Fry in deep hot fat until golden brown.

Shrimp Paste

Run a quart of boiled and picked shrimp through the meat grinder. Put in a saucepan with salt, pepper, mace and two heaping table-spoons of butter. Heat thor-oughly, and place into molds, pressing down very hard with a spoon, pouring melted butter over top. Place in refrigerator, and when cold slice and serve. This makes an excellent hors d'oeuvre or an addition to a to-mato salad.

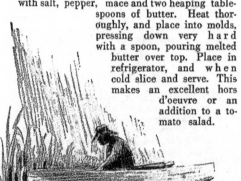

Shrimp and Rice Croquettes

1 cup rice
2 eggs
1 tablespoon butter
2 quarts shrimp

After cooking rice, add butter while still hot. Beat eggs slightly and add lastly the finely-minced shrimp. Season with salt and pepper to taste, roll in shapes, dip in bread or cracker crumbs and egg. Fry in deep fat.

Shrimps Caliente

1 pound fresh shrimps
2 large ripe tomatoes
1 stalk celery
¼ teaspoon paprika
½ teaspoon salt
  mayonnaise

Drop shrimps into boiling salt water and cook for ¼ hour. When cool, remove the shells and set aside to chill. Peel tomatoes and chop them fine, then add finely-chopped celery and combine with shrimps and toma-toes. Season liberally with paprika and salt and add sufficient mayonnaise to moisten. Mix well. Serve cold. This recipe may also be used for canned shrimps if desired.

Shrimp Salad With Peas

1 can of shrimp or one cupful of fresh
  shrimp
½ cup diced celery
2 hard cooked eggs
½ cup of peas

This may be served as a cold plate for five, with one tablespoon each of celery, chopped eggs and peas placed around the tablespoon of shrimps, in which case you would need al-most a whole cup of celery. Or you may mix all the ingredients lightly together with may-onnaise, first thinning the mayonnaise with cream and seasoning, and serve as a salad on crisp lettuce.

Oyster Pie

2 cups white sauce
  celery salt
1 teaspoon onion juice
1 dozen oysters

Into the white sauce put the celery salt, onion juice and oysters. Season to taste, cover with a rich pie crust and bake 20 min-utes in a hot (450° F.) oven, or until pie crust is done.

Recipe for white sauce will be found on page 24.

Did you eber see where de boatman live?
His house in de holler wid a roof like a sieve!
Boatman say he got one wish
Ef it gets much wetter he's a gonter be a fish.

Chesapeake Oyster Loaf

1 loaf French bread
2 dozen oysters
½ cup cream
1 tablespoon chopped celery
pepper
salt
2 drops tabasco sauce

Cut off the top crust of a loaf of French bread and scoop out the inside. Butter ⅓ of the portion you have scooped out and toast in the oven. Fry 2 dozen oysters in butter, add ½ cup cream, a tablespoon of chopped celery, pepper, salt and two drops of tabasco sauce and toasted bread. Fill the hollowed loaf with this mixture, cover with top crust and bake twenty minutes, basting frequently with the liquor from your oysters, slice and serve hot.

Oysters Louisiane

1 dozen oysters
3 tablespoons butter
2 tablespoons red pepper, chopped
2 teaspoons chopped onions
3 tablespoons flour
few grains cayenne
½ cup parmesan cheese
salt and pepper to taste

Parboil the oysters, remove from pan, reserve the liquor and add enough water to make 1½ cups. Melt the butter and fry the onion and red pepper in it. Add the flour to the onion and pepper and blend; then gradually pour on the liquor and stir constantly. Bring to the boiling point and season. Arrange the oysters in a casserole. Pour the liquid over them, add the grated cheese and bake in oven until thoroughly heated.

Lobster Thermidor

4 cups lobster meat, broken in small pieces
1 pound fresh mushrooms or 1 large can
1 cup sauterne
1 pint rich cream
2 egg yolks
1 tablespoon flour
2 tablespoons butter
bread crumbs
parmesan cheese
paprika

Sauté mushrooms in the butter. Cover tightly while cooking. Season with the wine and add the rich cream to which the beaten egg yolks have been added. Thicken with flour. When smooth add the lobster. Place in buttered ramekin, or lobster shell which has been cut lengthwise. Dot with butter, sprinkle with paprika and bread crumbs mixed with the parmesan cheese. Place in oven, bake until a delicate brown.

Fried Oysters à la Norfolk

1 quart oysters
2 eggs
cracker crumbs

Wash and drain the oysters. Beat the eggs. Dip the oysters into the cracker crumbs, then into the egg, and then back into the crumbs. Have the fat hot and fry the oysters quickly. Drain on brown paper.

Browned Oysters

1 quart oysters
4 tablespoons butter
1½ tablespoons flour
juice of one lemon
salt and pepper
Worcestershire sauce

Remove the oysters from their juice and drain. Dredge them in flour and brown them in two tablespoons of the butter. Remove them from the pan and strain the juice through a colander or sieve. Make a brown sauce of the remaining butter and flour, add the juice from the cooked oysters. Add the lemon juice and a dash of Worcestershire sauce, pour over the oysters and serve.

Lobster à la Newburgh

2 cups boiled lobster meat
2 tablespoons butter
1 cup Madeira or sherry wine
1 cup cream
2 egg yolks
¼ teaspoon salt
dash cayenne

Melt the butter in a saucepan and add the lobster, which has been cut in small pieces; cover and let simmer slowly for 5 minutes, then add the wine and cook 3 minutes. Beat the egg yolks and to them add the cream, beat together and add to the lobster. Shake the pan until the mixture is thickened. If the mixture is stirred it will break up the lobster. This dish curdles quickly and should be made just in time to serve immediately.

Dar was a terrapin and a toad
Both come up de new - cut road,
And eb'ry time de toad did sing
De terrapin cut de pigeon wing.

Royal Poincianna Pompano With Shrimp Stuffing

2 cups cooked shrimp
2 eggs
1 cup rich cream
1 boned pompano
½ cup chopped mushrooms
¼ cup sherry wine
pepper, salt and paprika

Clean the shrimp and put through the meat grinder. Beat the egg and half of the cream together. Mix the shrimp, mushrooms and seasoning together and stir in the cream and egg. Stir to a smooth paste. Put the mixture on one half of the pompano. Sew the two halves of the fish together and put in a baking dish. Pour over the fish the remaining cream and bake in a moderate oven for 45 minutes. Serve garnished with sliced cucumbers which have been marinated in French dressing.

Fish Cakes

2 cups cold boiled fish, flaked
2 cups mashed potatoes
1 tablespoon butter
1 egg, beaten
salt and pepper

Any fresh fish that is suitable for boiling may be used though codfish is preferred. Mix all the ingredients together—shape into round flat cakes and dredge in flour. Then fry in butter on both sides and serve with tomato sauce, recipe page 24.

Roe Herring

Cover the herring with cold water and soak overnight. Drain. Roll fish lightly in flour and place in a baking pan. Dot with butter and cook in hot oven (400° F.) until tender. Place on a hot platter; serve with a little melted butter poured over the fish. Garnish with parsley and sliced lemon.

Broiled Spanish Mackerel
(Baltimore Style)

Wash the mackerel and split in half. Season the fish with pepper and salt and place on a well-greased broiler in a broiling oven (550° F.). Broil on both sides until tender. Place on a hot platter and sprinkle with cayenne and serve with a sauce made of three tablespoons melted butter and juice of ½ lemon.

Diamond Back Terrapin Stew
(Chesapeake Bay Style)

3 terrapin (large)
6 hard cooked eggs
3 tablespoons flour
½ grated nutmeg
1 onion, sliced
½ cup butter
1 lemon, juice and rind
2 stalks celery
2 cups cooking sherry
1 tablespoon Worcestershire sauce
soup stock
red pepper and salt

Drop the live terrapin into boiling water and let stand for 5 minutes. Remove from the water, rub the skin off the feet, tail and head with a towel, drawing the head out with a skewer. Clip off the claws. Scrub the shell with boiling water. Break shell apart with sharp axe. Remove meat and liver. Discard gall bladder, heart, sandbag and entrails. Cut the liver in thin slices. Take out the eggs, remove film, and set eggs aside in cold water. Combine egg yolks, onion, celery and flour and soup stock (enough to cover meat), add the lemon, nutmeg, terrapin eggs and meat. Then add the cream, sherry wine, Worcestershire sauce and seasonings. Add the chopped egg whites and enough hot milk to thin out if the stew becomes too thick. Let simmer in a double boiler until meat drops from bones (about 15 minutes). Remove all the bones before serving. Serve in a chafing dish with toast on the side.

Fillets of Flounder

5 flounder fillets
3 tablespoons butter
1 cup milk
bread crumbs (sifted)
1 egg
1 cup tomato sauce
salt and pepper

Combine the egg, milk and salt and pepper and soak the fish in this mixture fifteen minutes. Dip each fillet in the bread crumbs. Allow frying pan with butter to become hot before placing fillets in it. Fry on both sides until browned, then pour tomato sauce over all, recipe for tomato sauce on page 24.

As I was gwain long de road,
Pon a stump dar sat a toad.
De tadpole winked at pollywog's
*   dauter*
And kicked de bullfrog plump in
*   de water.*

French Dressing

4 tablespoons pure olive oil, in which a
  clove of garlic has soaked
1⅓ tablespoons tarragon vinegar
¼ teaspoon salt
⅛ teaspoon white pepper

Mix the salt and pepper together; add
some of the oil and stir. Add the vinegar,
and then the remaining oil.

Mayonnaise Dressing

2 hard cooked yolks of egg
1 raw yolk of egg
½ teaspoon mustard
½ teaspoon salt (scant)
½ tablespoon vinegar (large)
  juice of ½ lemon
½ cup olive oil
  paprika

Mash and work smooth the hard cooked
yolks of egg; stir in with tablespoon the raw
yolk of egg and mustard; work smooth. Add
the oil by the tablespoonful and when half
of the oil has been used, add vinegar and
lemon juice, working them in very slowly.
Add salt and paprika and slowly work in the
remaining oil. If a greater quantity of mayonnaise is desired, continue to add oil, lemon and vinegar until the original quantity is
almost doubled. Use only a tablespoon in
working this dressing.

Richmond Sour Cream Dressing

3 tablespoons vinegar
1½ tablespoons sugar
½ pint sour cream
1 teaspoon salt
1 teaspoon dry mustard
  dash paprika

Partly whip the cream, mix together the
other ingredients and add slowly to the whipping cream and then beat until stiff. Serve
on tomatoes. This is very good on chopped
cabbage.

Horseradish Sauce

2 tablespoons finely chopped onion
2 heaping tablespoons butter
2 egg yolks
1 cup cream, milk or soup stock
½ cup freshly grated horseradish

Melt butter and cook onion until done, add
the cream or milk and cook for several minutes. Strain through a fine sieve and pour
onto the well beaten egg yolks, place in a
double boiler and cook until thick, stirring
constantly. Add the horseradish and serve
with meats and fish.

Sing, sing! Darkies, sing—
Don't you hear the banjo ring, ring, ring?
Sing, sing! Darkies, sing—
Sing for de white folks, sing!
  —OLD MINSTREL SONG

Hollandaise Sauce Supreme

4 egg yolks
½ cup melted butter
¼ teaspoon salt
  one dash pepper
2 tablespoons lemon juice

Beat the egg yolks, and slowly add the
melted butter, salt and pepper. Put in a
double boiler and cook, stirring all the time,
until the sauce thickens. Remove from the
fire immediately and stir in the lemon juice.
This is a sauce that must be used as soon
as it is finished. Should this sauce separate
it may be brought together again if a small
amount of hot thin cream sauce is added.
Serve on vegetables.

Sour Cream Dressing

½ teaspoon mustard
2 tablespoons sugar
  dash of paprika
1 tablespoon flour
1 tablespoon butter
¼ cup vinegar
¼ cup water
1 cup sour cream
1 egg yolk

Mix the seasonings, add the flour and sugar, add the vinegar and water, cook in double boiler until thickened, stirring constantly.
Add the egg yolk and butter, cook a few
minutes longer. Cool. Whip the sour cream
and add to above mixture. Serve on lettuce,
dandelion salad, asparagus, cucumbers, or
fish.

Mint Tea

2 cups sugar
½ cup water
  grated rind of one orange
  juice of 6 oranges
6 glasses of very strong tea
  several sprays of mint

Boil the sugar, water and orange rind
about 5 minutes. Remove from the fire and
add the crushed leaves of mint and let cool.
Into the tea put the orange juice. Half fill
the iced tea glasses with crushed ice, add the
tea and sweeten to taste with the mint syrup.
A sprig of mint or a slice of orange may be
added to each glass as a garnish.

Cornbread Dressing

3 eggs, beaten
2 cups buttermilk
3 tablespoons melted shortening
2 teaspoons salt
2½ cups sifted meal
3 teaspoons baking powder
1 teaspoon soda, dissolved in
1 tablespoon water·
3 tablespoons melted butter
  hot water
  onion, parsley, celery, salt, pepper as desired

To the well-beaten eggs add the milk, shortening and salt. Sift together the baking powder and meal and slowly stir into the egg mixture, adding enough of the meal to make a medium batter. Beat well. Dissolve soda in 1 tablespoon of water and add to the batter. Pour the batter into a greased shallow baking pan. Bake in a hot oven (425° F.) about 20 to 25 minutes, or until bread begins to brown.

Allow bread to cool; then break into small pieces, crumbling the crust well. Add the melted butter and season with onion, celery, salt and pepper or any other desired seasonings. Moisten well with hot water. Fill ·turkey or hen and roast as required.

Oyster Stuffing

¾ cup butter
2 tablespoons chopped onions
3 tablespoons chopped parsley
1½ cups chopped celery
6 cups soft bread crumbs
1 pint oysters, chopped
  salt and pepper to taste

Melt the butter and in it cook the onion, parsley and celery. Add the bread crumbs, heat well. Add the chopped oysters and seasoning.

Apple Stuffing

1 small onion
6 tablespoons butter
1 cup chopped celery
3 cups stale bread crumbs
4 cups chopped apples
2 tablespoons chopped parsley
4 tablespoons seeded raisins
  salt and pepper

Chop onion and brown in the butter; add celery, bread crumbs, apple and parsley; season with salt and pepper and then add raisins.

Crow in de corn field,
Nigger in de patch;
Chicken in de egg-shell,
'Bout ready ·ter hatch.

Chestnut Stuffing

1 egg
1 pound chestnuts
¼ cup chicken fat
¼ cup butter
2 cups chopped celery
½ cup chopped onions
6 cups bread crumbs
  parsley, chopped fine
  salt and pepper

Boil the chestnuts for about twenty minutes. Remove the shells and brown skins while the nuts are still hot. Melt the chicken fat and add the butter. Cook the celery and onion in this for a few minutes, add a few sprigs of chopped parsley and the egg, bread crumbs and chestnuts; season to taste with salt and pepper. Stir mixture until it is thoroughly hot. Wipe the chicken or turkey dry inside, sprinkle with salt and fill with hot stuffing. This recipe is sufficient for a ten-pound turkey and should be reduced to about half for a five-pound chicken.

Bread Stuffing

Soak 1 quart of stale bread in cold water and squeeze dry. Season with the following ingredients: 1 teaspoon salt, ⅛ teaspoon black pepper, ¼ teaspoon poultry seasoning, 1 teaspoon chopped parsley, ½ teaspoon onion, chopped fine (onions may be omitted if desired). Add 2 tablespoons melted fat and mix thoroughly. Beat 1 egg lightly and add to above mixture. Then add heart, liver and gizzard of fowl or pork or liver sausage chopped fine and partially boiled.

South Carolina Scrapple

Select three pounds of bony pieces of pork. For each pound of meat use a quart of water and simmer until the meat drops from the bone. Remove the meat from bones carefully being certain to get all the small pieces. Bring the remaining broth to boiling point, adding sufficient water to make two cups. Slowly add two cups of corn meal and cook until the mixture becomes a thick mush, stirring constantly. Chop the meat and put it in the pot; also add salt, pepper and the juice of an onion. Cook for two minutes, stirring constantly. Pour the hot scrapple into a dampened oblong pan. Let stand until cold and firm. Slice and brown in hot skillet. If the scrapple is rich with fat, no more fat ·is required for frying.

Chestnut Soufflé

1 pound chestnuts
¼ cup sugar
½ cup milk
1 tablespoon butter
3 eggs

Boil and shell the chestnuts. Then boil them in sweetened milk and butter until tender. Put chestnuts through a sieve and let cool. Separate the yolks from the whites. Beat each separately. Add chestnut puree and vanilla to the yolks. Fold in whites and pour into a buttered dish. Place in a moderate oven (350° F.) until soufflé is a light brown.

Jean Lafitte Salad

1 cup cold diced meat
6 tablespoons cold diced potatoes (cooked)
6 tablespoons cold diced cooked carrots
6 tablespoons cold cooked string beans
½ cup French dressing
2 chopped sweet pickles
1 hard cooked egg, chopped
½ cup mayonnaise
Mix the vegetables and the meats with the French dressing. Let it stand for one hour and then add the pickles, egg and mayonnaise. Serve chilled on a lettuce leaf.

Grapefruit Ring

2½ tablespoons gelatin
½ cup cold water
1½ cups sugar
1½ cups grapefruit juice
½ cup orange juice
¼ cup lemon juice
1 cup hot water
Soak gelatin in ½ cup cold water 5 minutes. Boil sugar and hot water 3 minutes or until clear. Pour over the soaked gelatin and stir until dissolved. Let it cool and then add grapefruit, orange and lemon juice, a pinch of salt and pour into ring. Set aside in cool place for several hours to congeal.

Cinnamon Apple Salad

6 firm apples
1 cup water
1 cup cinnamon drops (the old-fashioned red cinnamon candy)
2 cups sugar
Peel and core the apples. Place the apples in an open pan on top of the stove, pour over them the water, cinnamon drops and the sugar. Cook slowly, turning the apples frequently in the syrup. When the apples are done remove from the syrup with a strainer and place on a crisp lettuce leaf. Fill the centers with chopped nuts, cream cheese and mayonnaise.

Chicken-and-Fruit Salad

3 cups white meat of chicken from a boiled fowl
1 orange
1 apple
15 large grapes
15 salted almonds
1 banana
1 cup mayonnaise
Cut chicken in small pieces. Remove seeds from orange sections and cut in half. Cut grapes in half, removing seeds. Split almonds. Slice banana. Add the mayonnaise and mix all the ingredients slowly but thoroughly. Serve chilled on lettuce leaf.

Avocado or Alligator Pear Salad

Chill three alligator pears. Peel, cut in halves and remove stones, cut in cubes. Marinate in French dressing (page 24). Serve on crisp lettuce. Sprinkle with chopped almonds.

Poinsettia Salad

Place a lettuce leaf on a salad plate and a slice of canned pineapple in the center. Cut a pimiento into ½ inch strips and place one end in the center of the pineapple letting the other end extend to the rim. Arrange the strips all around like the spokes of a wheel, make a soft paste of cream cheese moistened with French dressing and season with salt and paprika. Place a small ball of this mixture in the center of the pineapple and you will have the effect of a poinsettia flower. Serve with French dressing (see page 24).

Mississippi Cole Slaw

1 cup mayonnaise
1 head solid cabbage
1 cup chopped cold tongue
1 cup cold chopped ham
1 green pepper
1 red pepper
½ chopped onion
1 egg white
Slice cabbage as for cole slaw. Mix all the ingredients together and add to the cabbage. Thin the mayonnaise with the beaten white of one egg and add to the cabbage slaw. Sugar can be added if not sweet enough.

Florida Guspachy Salad

4 tomatoes
1 cucumber
2 green peppers
1 tablespoon onion, finely chopped
½ teaspoon Worcestershire sauce
½ teaspoon A-1 sauce
salt, pepper, paprika
¼ teaspoon dry mustard
1 teaspoon sugar
1 pilot cracker (hard tack)
2 tablespoons sour cream
Peel cucumber and tomatoes and slice thin. Also slice the green pepper very thin. Drain off their juices. Soak the cracker in cold water for about three minutes and squeeze dry. Place a layer of the vegetable mixture in a bowl, and sprinkle with the chopped onion and cracker. Spread with sour cream to which all the above spices and sauces have been added. Repeat until all ingredients are used. Place on ice for about three hours; serve on crisp lettuce leaves.

I's got a girl in Afriky,
She's az purty az can be.

White Sauce

2 tablespoons butter
2 tablespoons flour
1½ cups milk
½ teaspoon salt

Melt the butter without browning, add the flour and salt and cook until it is well blended. Add the milk slowly, stirring all the while to keep from scorching, and when it reaches the boiling point remove from fire and beat well, or until creamy.

Tomato Sauce

3 tablespoons butter
3 tablespoons flour
1 cup canned tomatoes
1 tablespoon sugar
¼ teaspoon cloves
½ teaspoon allspice
    salt and pepper to taste

Make the same as you would a white sauce above but use the tomatoes in place of the milk. The tomatoes may be strained if desired. This is a very good sauce for veal cutlets, fish, rice or for baked macaroni.

Mushroom Sauce

1 medium sized can mushrooms
4 tablespoons butter
3 tablespoons flour
1 cup rich milk or thin cream

Sauté mushrooms in butter, add flour slowly and brown slightly, add the thin cream and cook until it thickens. Pour over steak or chicken.

Foaming Sauce for Fruit Puddings

1 cup butter
2 cups powdered sugar
⅓ cup sherry wine
2 egg whites
¼ cup boiling water

Beat the butter to a soft substance and gradually cream the sugar into it. Add the unbeaten whites of eggs gradually and then the wine. Beat well. When this is a light smooth mass gradually add the boiling water, beating all the while. Place the bowl in a basin of hot water and stir about 2 minutes until you have a frothy foaming sauce.

Hard Sauce

½ cup butter
1 cup confectioner's sugar
1 teaspoon vanilla extract or brandy

Cream the butter and sugar together and work in the flavoring. Serve cold with hot puddings or apple dumplings.

Frozen Mint Ice for Roast Lamb

5 sprays of fresh mint
½ cup lemon juice
½ cup confectioner's sugar
4 cups water
¼ teaspoon essence of peppermint extract
    green vegetable coloring

Wash and pick mint from stems and soak in lemon juice for ½ hour, strain. Dissolve ½ cup of sugar in 4 cups of water and add to the strained lemon and mint juice. Just before freezing add the green vegetable coloring and peppermint extract. Freeze as a water ice.

Brandy Sauce for Fritters
(For Puddings, Also)

¾ cup water
½ cup sherry or brandy or both
    sugar to taste
½ teaspoon grated nutmeg

Mix the ingredients and bring to the boiling point, serving very hot.

Raisin Sauce for Ham

1 cup raisins
1 cup water
5 cloves
¾ cup brown sugar
1 teaspoon cornstarch
¼ teaspoon salt
    pinch of pepper
1 tablespoon butter
1 tablespoon vinegar
¼ teaspoon Worcestershire sauce

Cover raisins with water, add cloves and simmer for ten minutes. Then add the sugar, cornstarch, salt and pepper which have already been mixed together. Stir until slightly thickened and then add the remaining ingredients.

Rhubarb Sauce

Wash the rhubarb and cut into one-inch pieces; cover with two cups of sugar to one quart of rhubarb. Stand aside for one hour. Use just enough water to moisten the sugar. Cook until rhubarb is tender. Serve cold. This is a delicious dish served with whipped cream.

Gwine down by de pars'nage,
Now Liza, you keep cool;
I hasn't got time to squeeze you,
I'se busy wid dis mule.

Glazed Baked Apples

8 apples
1 cup sugar
1 pint heavy cream
1 cup boiling water

Wash apples thoroughly, remove cores and skins from top of each apple, place in saucepan with one apple touching the other, with the peeled side up. Add the water and cook slowly, testing occasionally with a toothpick to see if they are soft. When done place in a baking dish, sprinkle with sugar and put in hot oven (425° F), basting with water in which they were originally cooked until tops are crisp, rich brown. Serve cold with heavy cream.

Captain Henry's Pickled Cherries

(From A-Way Down South)

Pit cherries, place in a large crock and cover with weak vinegar; let stand eight days, stirring twice each day. On the ninth day remove from the vinegar and drain. To each pint of cherries add one pint of sugar and replace in crock, letting stand for eight more days, stirring twice each day. At the end of the eighth day, place in sterile jars and seal. Serve with poultry and meats.

Stewed Kumquats and Prunes

6 kumquats, sliced thin
1 cup pitted prunes
¼ cup sugar
½ cup prune juice
½ cup orange juice

Wash 1 cup of prunes and soak them in cold water over night. Cook slowly in the water in which they were soaked until soft. Add ½ of the sugar and cook 5 minutes longer. Season with orange juice. Drain and pit the prunes. Add kumquats to the prune juice. Let simmer few minutes; add remaining sugar. Cook slowly until kumquats are tender, and add the prunes.

Spiced Cantaloupe

Peel rind and cut cantaloupe into one inch pieces. Soak over night in weak vinegar. To each seven pounds of fruit, add three pounds of sugar and eight sticks of cinnamon, one tablespoonful of whole cloves. Cook about an hour and one-half or until the fruit becomes transparent. Place in sterile jars and seal. Serve with fowl or meats.

Savannah Stewed Prunes

1 pound prunes
½ cup sugar
2 slices of lemon

Place the washed prunes and lemon in a double boiler with very little water, and sprinkle with the sugar. Let steam slowly until thoroughly cooked. Serve with cream.

India Relish

½ peck ripe tomatoes
½ dozen sweet peppers (yellow, cut fine)
2 large onions

Boil these for 25 minutes, and drain. Add ½ ounce mustard seed, 2 tablespoons salt, 1 quart vinegar and boil. Pour into a bag and drain. Boil together ½ ounce celery seed, ½ ounce whole allspice, ½ ounce cloves, ½ teaspoon cinnamon, 3 bay leaves, 1½ pounds sugar. Add tomatoes and boil all together several minutes and pour into jars while hot. This quantity will make 5 to 6 pint jars.

Pepper Relish

16 sweet red peppers
16 sweet green peppers
10 small onions

Chop these very fine, and place in a bowl. Pour boiling water over them and let stand 5 minutes. Drain off the water and again cover with boiling water and let stand 10 minutes. Pour into a muslin bag and allow to drain over night. Add 1 quart of sour vinegar, 1½ cups of sugar, 2½ teaspoons salt, and boil together for 20 minutes. While hot, pour into air-tight jars and seal.

Apple Chutney

(It Tastes Even Better Than It Reads)

2 quarts apples, cut in small pieces
2 pounds granulated sugar
2 cups seeded raisins
rind of 2 oranges, finely chopped
½ cup strong vinegar
⅓ teaspoon ground cloves
1 cup pecan meats, chopped fine

Boil all the ingredients together until apples and nuts are tender. Place in sterile jars and scald. Delicious with chicken or game.

Baked Bananas

6 bananas
2 tablespoons melted butter
2 tablespoons lemon juice
⅓ cup sugar

Remove skins from bananas, cut in halves lengthwise, and place in shallow pan. Mix the melted butter, sugar and lemon juice and pour over the bananas. Bake in a slow oven (250° F.) 30 minutes.

Fried Peaches

6 peaches
2 tablespoons butter
12 teaspoons brown sugar

Pare and split the peaches. Melt the butter in an iron skillet and drop in the peaches. Fill the hollows with the brown sugar and let simmer until well cooked. Serve with either whipped cream or ice cream or meats.

Here comes Sal with a snicker and a grin,
Ground hog gravy all over her chin.

Grapefruit and Pineapple Marmalade

1 grapefruit
1 pineapple
1 lemon
    sugar

Pare and shred the pineapple, cut grape fruit and lemon in quarters, and then in thin slices. Measure fruit and cover with water, 3 pints of water to 1 pint of fruit. Set aside until next day. Let it boil 3 or more hours, or until rind is very tender. Set aside until next day. Measure and add an equal amount of sugar. Let boil until a drop jells on a cold plate.

Baked Oranges

4 thin-skinned seedless oranges
2 cups sugar
1 cup water oranges were boiled in

Wash oranges, place in kettle and cover with boiling water. Cook until tender when tried with a fork. Remove from the water, cut in half and arrange in a baking dish. Cook together the sugar and orange water for five minutes, pour over the oranges and dot each orange with a piece of butter. Cover the baking dish and bake in a hot oven about one-half hour, or until the oranges become transparent. Serve with roast duck.

Guava Jelly

Select acid guavas. Wash well, remove blossom end and slice. For each pound of fruit, add 2 pints of water and cook until soft. Allow to stand until cold. Pour into a bag and strain, pressing to extract the juice well. Strain again through a flannel jelly bag.

Test the juice for pectin by the following method: Pour a teaspoonful of fruit juice into a clean cup. Add a teaspoonful of grain alcohol of 95% strength. Mix by gently shaking; pour into a spoon. If the precipitated pectin is a solid clot add one measure of sugar for one of fruit; if the pectin is not well collected decrease the sugar.

Bring the juice to a boil and add sugar according to pectin test. Continue to boil to the jellying point, or about 225½ degrees, indicated by the flaking from the spoon.

Orange-Marmalade

6 large oranges
3 quarts cold water
2 tablespoons lemon juice
4 cups sugar

Cut oranges in half, scoop out juice and pulp. Boil rind until tender in enough cold water to cover; drain, cool, remove all the white part. Cut yellow into strips, add juice, pulp, sugar and water. Boil slowly 2 hours or until thick. Place into jelly glasses.

PAPAYA RECIPES

Select the melon at a mature but unripe stage. Boil or steam and add a little lime juice. This makes a delicious French sauce. The unripe fruit may be used like any other melon in pickles or preserves. It combines nicely with other fruits for marmalades and jellies. It is very good for sherbet. As a breakfast food it needs no additions. As a dessert it is perfect.

Papaya Cocktail

Place balls of papaya in cocktail glasses. Add a French dressing made of lime juice, a little sugar and salt. Garnish with a sprig of mint.

Papaya Canapé

Toasted rounds of bread, buttered and sprinkled with cinnamon and sugar, may be topped with a round of papaya sprinkled with lemon juice or toasted rounds with papaya crossed with pimento strips (red).

Baked Papaya

(1) Cut mature but unripe papaya in halves lengthwise. Add a little sugar and orange, lime or lemon juice, or a little cinnamon in place of the juice. Bake 20 minutes and serve immediately on taking from the oven.

(2)
4 cups ripened papaya pulp
1 cup shredded cocoanut
1 orange, pulp, juice and grated rind
1 cup sugar
4 eggs
4 cups milk

Make a custard of the egg, milk, sugar and orange. Place papaya and cocoanut in a baking dish. Pour over the custard and bake in a moderate oven.

Jelly Meringue

1 glass firm jelly
2 egg whites
    pinch of salt

Beat 2 egg whites until quite stiff and able to stand by themselves, then add 1 glass of firm jelly, pinch of salt, and beat thoroughly. Use in place of whipped cream.

Me and my wife had a fallin' out.
Listen and I'll tell you what it's all about.
It ain't no lie, it's a natural born fact,
She wanted me to work on the railroad track.

Creole Stuffed Peppers

4 ears of corn
6 green peppers
4 tomatoes
1 small onion
1 tablespoon butter
6 green olives
salt and pepper to taste

Cut off tops and remove centers from peppers. Put in hot water and cook slowly for one half hour. Brown the onion in the butter, add the tomatoes and corn cut from the cob and let cook about 15 minutes. Just before removing from the fire add the chopped olives and salt. Stuff the peppers, cover with bread crumbs, dot with butter, bake in oven until the crumbs are well browned.

Artichokes

Trim the outer leaves from the artichoke and boil the artichoke in salt water for three quarters of an hour. Serve with hollandaise sauce or with melted butter.

Okra and Tomatoes

Take an equal quantity of young sliced okra and skinned tomatoes. Put them together in a pan, without water, adding a lump of butter, a finely chopped onion, some salt and pepper. Stew over a slow fire for one hour.

Old-Fashioned String Beans and Bacon

1 can string beans and liquid, or an equal amount of fresh beans
2 medium potatoes (cut into ½ inch dice)
¼ pound bacon (cut into ½ inch dice and well browned)
¼ teaspoon salt
1 cup water
pepper
1 small onion (left whole)

Put all ingredients into kettle and boil until the potatoes are soft (about 15 minutes).

Home-Baked Beans

1 pint navy beans
¼ pound fat salt pork
1 teaspoon mustard
½ teaspoon salt
1 tablespoon molasses
½ cup boiling water
1½ tablespoons sugar

Cover beans with cold water and soak for at least 12 hours, then change water and cook at slightly below boiling point until skins burst. To test beans take a few and expose to cold air, if shells burst they are done. Then drain and add pork, cut it in small strips and stick it in beans with tip exposed. Mix mustard, sugar, salt, pepper and water enough to cover beans. Bake in pot slowly, for six or seven hours removing lid for last hour to brown and crisp.

Hopping John

1 cup cooked rice
2 tablespoons butter
2 cups dried peas
¼ pound pork
Salt, pepper and butter

Soak peas overnight. The next day, cook peas until soft, being careful to keep them whole during the cooking. Cook the piece of pork with the peas to add flavor. When peas are cooked sufficiently, there should be only a small quantity of liquor left on them. Mix the cooked rice and peas together, season with salt, pepper and butter and serve with bread and butter.

Salsify (Oyster Plant)

Wash and scrape the oyster plant and immediately place in cold water with a little vinegar to prevent discoloring. Cut in pieces ½ inch wide and cook in boiling water until soft. Dip strips in beaten egg, sprinkle with salt, roll in cracker crumbs and fry in butter until brown.

Egg Plant

Pare egg plant, cut in slices. Sprinkle with salt, cover and let stand 1 hour to draw out juice. Dip in beaten eggs, then in bread crumbs. Fry in deep fat.

To Cook Okra

Wash well and trim stem end, leaving enough of the pod to keep the juices in so that the mucilage does not come out. Cover with boiling water and boil gently until tender. When half done add a little salt. When ready to serve, drain, pour into a hot dish and add melted butter sufficient to season. Lemon juice or vinegar can be added if desired.

Fried Okra

Select small, tender pods. Boil until tender, drain, season with salt and pepper, roll in egg, then in cracker crumbs. Fry in deep hot fat.

Candied Carrots

6 medium sized carrots
½ cup water
1 cup brown sugar
2 tablespoons butter

Boil carrots, scrape and cut them in strips as you would potatoes for French frying. Mix the other ingredients in a baking dish and warm to make a syrup. Place the carrots in this syrup so that it covers them entirely and bake until candied.

Fried Squash Cakes

Slice the squash very thin, being certain to slice it across. Place the slices in salt water, wipe them dry, sprinkle with salt and pepper, dip in flour, in beaten egg, and then in cracker crumbs. Repeat the process twice and then drop into pot of deep hot fat for frying. When they have been cooked through, drain on crumpled brown paper and serve.

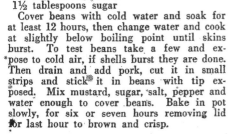

Corn Fritters

1 cup flour
1 teaspoon baking powder
½ teaspoon salt
1 egg
¼ cup milk
½ tablespoon butter
1 cup drained crushed corn

Mix the dry ingredients, gradually adding the milk and the well beaten egg, beat thoroughly and then add the melted butter and corn. Drop by spoonsful into hot deep fat and fry until well browned. Drain on brown paper.

Fruit Fritter Batter

1 cup flour
1 teaspoon sugar
½ teaspoon salt
2 eggs well beaten
⅔ cup milk

Mix the flour, sugar, and salt. Add milk slowly and then gradually add the eggs.

Apple, Peach, Apricot, or Pear Fritters

Cut fruit in pieces, dip in the fruit fritter batter above and fry in deep hot (375° F.) fat or butter about 3 to 5 minutes or until a golden brown. Then remove with skimmer, and place on crumpled soft paper to drain. Sprinkle with powdered sugar and serve with a lemon or other fruit juice sauce.

Orange Fritters

Peel oranges and separate sections. Remove the seeds; dip in batter and fry; serve as above.

Lemon Sauce for Fritters

½ cup sugar
3 teaspoons cornstarch
1 cup boiling water
½ lemon
1 tablespoon butter

Mix sugar and cornstarch in pan, stir in the boiling water; add butter, lemon juice, and grated lemon rind. Boil and stir until the mixture is transparent. Serve on fruit fritters. This sauce may also be used on puddings.

"Watermelon red, peaches sweet,
"Trout line callin' f'om de river's feet.
"Mockin' bird singin' 'e song so neat,
I's livin' easy! I's livin' high!"

Corn Bread Fritters

1 cup corn meal
1 cup flour
2 teaspoons baking powder
½ teaspoon salt
1 egg
  milk to make a stiff batter

Mix the meal, flour, salt and baking powder. Beat in the egg and add milk to make a stiff batter. Drop from a spoon into deep boiling fat and fry until golden brown. Drain on brown paper before serving. These fritters are delicious with soup.

Fresh Lima Beans

1 quart lima beans
1 tablespoon butter
½ teaspoon salt
2 tablespoons milk
2 tablespoons cream

Wash and pick over the beans. Cover with boiling water, adding salt and butter. Let simmer eighteen minutes; raise the heat and boil quickly until water has evaporated. Add the cream and milk and bring to a boil. Serve hot.

Curds and Cream

(A Louisiana Every-Meal Dish)

Set sour or raw milk in a crock or bowl until it becomes clabber. Pour slowly into a curd press until press is full. Place press in pan and let drain over night. Turn onto a flat dish, grate nutmeg freely over the top and serve with heavy sweet cream, more grated nutmeg and sugar.

Honey may be used in place of sugar.

A colander lined with a double thickness of cheesecloth may be used in place of the curd press.

Creamed Green Peas

Cook two cups of shelled green peas quickly in boiling water until tender. Add one teaspoon salt, level, drain off water and add one-half cup of cream. Slowly bring to a boil and serve.

Stuffed Squash

Clean six scalloped squash. Boil in cold water until tender but not too soft. Drain and scoop out about half the insides, leaving enough pulp to keep shape of squash; drain as much liquid as possible from the scooped-out portion. Press through a sieve and add one tablespoon butter, one tablespoon heavy cream, salt and pepper and let simmer four minutes. Fill shells with mixture and place in baking pan. Sprinkle with sifted bread crumbs, chopped parsley and melted butter. Pour half a cup of warm water in bottom of pan and bake in hot oven (400° F.) until squash are well browned on top. Lift out with a spatula and serve at once.

Eggs New Orleans

2½ cups tomatoes
1 small onion, chopped
½ green pepper, chopped
1 teaspoon sugar
¾ cup bread crumbs
½ cup celery
4 eggs
½ cup American cheese, grated
    salt, pepper and bay leaf

Cook tomatoes, pepper, onion and seasoning together for ten minutes, remove bay leaf, add bread crumbs and place in casserole. Break the eggs on top and sprinkle with salt and pepper and cover with grated cheese. Bake in a moderate (350° F.) oven until the eggs have set and the cheese has melted.

Eggs Ponce de Leon

6 hard cooked eggs
2 cups tomato juice
½ cup chopped celery
¼ cup chopped green peppers
½ cup mushrooms
1 tablespoon flour
1 tablespoon butter
½ onion, diced
½ teaspoon Worcestershire sauce
½ cup white sauce
    salt and pepper to taste

Chop the whites of the eggs, and mash the yolks. Brown the onion in the butter, add the flour and blend well. Put in the tomato juice and the peppers and cook slowly until done. Add the mushrooms, the seasoning and the Worcestershire. When this is all done add the white sauce, the egg yolks and the chopped egg whites. Place in buttered casserole. Sprinkle with cracker crumbs, dot with butter, and brown in the oven. Serve hot.

Chicken Liver Ramekins

1 cup raw chicken livers
1 tablespoon butter
½ tablespoon cream
2 tablespoons milk
3 eggs
½ cup mushrooms
    chopped parsley, salt, pepper, and red pepper

Press the liver through a colander, beat the yolks of eggs and then add the cream and milk, butter, salt, pepper, parsley, and mushrooms. Place the mixture in buttered molds and cover with greased paper. Put the mold in a pan of water and let them bake from 15 to 20 minutes.

Sal one day she gave a sigh,
Her mouth would hold a pumpkin pie,
A bushel of potatoes, two quarts of gin;
She gaped one day and her head fell in.

Biltmore Golden Rod Eggs

3 hard cooked eggs
1 cup white sauce
6 slices toast
    parsley to garnish

Separate yolks and whites of eggs, chop the whites finely and add to the white sauce. Pour over 4 pieces of toast. Mash yolks through a strainer and sprinkle over the top. Cut the remaining toast in triangular shapes and place on side of dish. Garnish with parsley.

Recipe for white sauce will be found on page 24.

Eggs Stuffed with Chicken Livers

2 chicken livers
½ teaspoon onion juice
2 tablespoons butter
4 hard cooked eggs
1 teaspoon chopped parsley
    Worcestershire sauce to taste
¼ cup grated cheese
    salt and pepper

Clean the livers very thoroughly, chop them finely and sprinkle with onion juice; fry in butter. Cut the eggs in half, remove yolks and put the whites aside. Force the yolks through a sieve, add parsley, salt, pepper and Worcestershire sauce to taste, then mix with the chicken livers. Refill whites with the mixture, sprinkle with grated cheese and bake until cheese melts. Serve with toast and a little tomato sauce. (See page 24.)

Creole Omelet

1 tablespoon butter
4 eggs
2 tablespoons olive oil
2 onions
4 tomatoes
2 green peppers
1 teaspoon salt
½ teaspoon paprika

Beat the eggs in a bowl with four tablespoons of water. When the butter is heated to a light brown, turn in the eggs. As they brown, lift the edges with a spatula and let the uncooked part run under. When the omelet is brown underneath and creamy on top, fold once and slip onto a hot platter, surrounding it with Creole sauce. The sauce is made as follows: Heat two tablespoons of olive oil. Cut into this the onions, tomatoes and peppers. Add salt and paprika, cook slowly till wanted for the omelet.

Tallahassee Hush Puppies

Embodied in the title of this recipe is a most interesting story.

Years ago (in some sections it is still the custom) the negroes of Tallahassee, Florida, that quaint southern capital, would congregate on warm fall evenings for cane grindings. Some of them would feed the sugar cane to a one-mule treadmill while others poured the juice into a large kettle where it was boiled to sugar. After their work was completed, they would gather around an open fire, over which was suspended an iron pot in which fish and corn pones were cooked in fat.

The negroes were said to have a certain way of making these corn pones which were unusually delicious and appetizing. While the food was sizzling in the pot, the darkies would engage in rather weird conversations, spellbinding each other with "tall" stories of panther and bear hunts. On the outer edge of the circle of light reflected by the fire would sit their hounds, their ears pricked for strange sounds and their noses raised to catch a whiff of the savory odor of the frying fish and pones. If the talking ceased for a moment, a low whine of hunger from the dogs would attract the attention of the men, and subconsciously a hand would reach for some of the corn pone which had been placed on a slab of bark to cool. The donor would break off a piece of the pone and toss it to a hungry dog, with the abstract murmur, "Hush, puppy!"

The effect of this gesture on the hounds was always instantaneous and the negroes attributed the result to the remarkable flavor of what eventually became known as "The Tallahassee Hush Puppy."

2 cups corn meal
2 teaspoons baking powder
1 teaspoon salt
1½ cups sweet milk
½ cup water
1 large onion, chopped fine

Sift the dry ingredients together and add the milk and water. Stir in the chopped onion. Add more meal or milk as may be necessary to form a soft but workable dough. With the hands, mold pieces of the dough into pones (oblong cakes, about 5 inches long and 3 inches wide, and about ¾ of an inch thick). Fry in deep hot fat or oil until well browned.

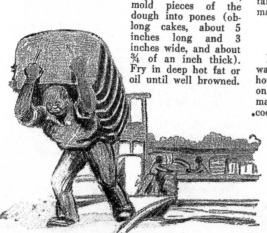

Hominy or Grits

1 cup hominy
4 cups boiling water
1 teaspoon salt
1 tablespoon butter

Pour the hominy into the hot water and stir until it comes to a boiling point. Then lower the flame and let simmer slowly for one hour, stirring frequently. When ready to serve, put the butter into the hominy and beat well for a few minutes.

Southern Corn Custard

2 cups canned corn
3 eggs
2 tablespoons melted butter
2 cups milk
½ teaspoon sugar
  salt and pepper to taste
  cracker crumbs

Beat the eggs well, add to the corn. Melt the butter and with the milk add to the corn and eggs. Stir well. Add the seasoning and sugar. Pour into a well-buttered casserole; sprinkle with cracker crumbs, dot with butter and bake in a very slow oven (250° F.) about 40 minutes or until custard has set.

Corn Pudding

3 tablespoons corn meal
1 tablespoon salt
½ teaspoon paprika
½ cup cold milk
2 cups hot milk
1 tablespoon butter
2 cups fresh corn pulp
2 eggs

Stir corn meal with salt, paprika and cold milk. Then stir into hot milk. Cook and stir over boiling water until the mixture thickens. Remove from the fire and stir in the other ingredients. Turn into a buttered baking dish suitable to send to the table. Set in a pan of boiling water and cook slowly until the center is firm. Serve hot with the meat course. A tablespoon of chopped green or red pepper may be added if desired.

Hoe Cake

Moisten salted corn meal with scalding water or milk. Allow it to stand for an hour. Put two or three teaspoons of this on hot greased griddle. Smooth it out to make cakes one-half inch thick and let it cook. When one side is done turn over and brown the other. Serve very hot for breakfast. This dish goes well with sausage.

Roll dat bale, roll dat cotton,
De Lord is good, your sins will be
forgotten.

Sally Lunn Hot Bread

3 eggs
4 cups of flour
2 tablespoons sugar
1 yeast cake
1 cup milk
½ teaspoon salt
2 tablespoons butter

Place sugar, eggs, milk, salt, and butter in a double boiler and scald. Let cool and add yeast which has been dissolved in a ¼ cup of warm water. When cold, add flour, put in bowl and cover with a cloth and put away to rise. When twice its bulk, knead and put in pan to rise again. When light roll out on floured board. Cut with a biscuit cutter, place in greased pan and bake in hot oven (400° F.) fifteen minutes.

Good Old Southern Popovers

3 eggs
1½ cups of milk
1½ cups of flour
½ teaspoon salt

Sift flour and salt into a bowl. Beat eggs and add the milk to them and stir gradually into the flour to make a smooth batter, then beat thoroughly with egg beater; put in hot greased muffin tins two thirds full of mixture. Bake in hot oven (450° F.) half hour, then in moderate oven (300° F.) fifteen minutes, until brown.

Southern Spoon Bread

2 cups corn meal
1½ cups sweet milk
2 cups boiling water
1 teaspoon salt
3 large tablespoons butter (melted)
3 eggs

Sift the meal three times and dissolve in the boiling water, mix until it is smooth and free from any lumps. Add the melted butter and salt. Thin with the milk.

Separate the eggs; beat until light; add the yolks and then the whites. Pour into a buttered baking dish and bake in a moderate oven (350° F.) about 30 minutes.

This should be served in the dish in which it is baked.

Richmond Corn Cakes

1 cup crushed canned corn
½ cup milk
2 teaspoons sugar
2 eggs, well beaten
¾ cup flour
1 tablespoon baking powder
pinch of salt

To the corn add milk, sugar and eggs. Mix and sift flour, baking powder and salt. Combine the mixtures, drop by teaspoons in buttered muffin pans. Bake in moderate oven.

Four o'Clock Tea Scones

2 cups pastry flour
2 tablespoons sugar
1 teaspoon salt
4 teaspoons baking powder
3 tablespoons butter
1 egg, beaten light
½ cup milk
sugar for dredging

Sift together the dry ingredients twice and work in the butter with a pastry mixer. Add a half cup of milk to the egg and gradually use in mixing the dough, using more milk if needed. Turn on a floured board, knead slightly, pat and roll into a sheet, cut into rounds, set in buttered tin, brush over with melted butter and dredge with sugar. Bake in a hot oven (400° F.) about fifteen minutes. Serve with tea or cocoa.

Miss Lee's Southern Corn Bread

1 cup white cornmeal
¼ cup wheat flour
1 teaspoon baking powder
½ teaspoon salt
1 beaten egg
½ cup milk
1 tablespoon melted butter

Sift together the dry ingredients; combine the milk with the egg and add to the dry ingredients. Add the melted butter and pour batter into a well-greased pan. Bake in a hot oven (425° F.) about 25 minutes.

Corn Meal Muffins

1 cup corn meal
2 cups white flour
4 teaspoons baking powder
½ teaspoon salt
½ cup sugar
1 cup milk
2 eggs, beaten
2 tablespoons melted butter

Sift all the dry ingredients into a bowl; add the milk, mixing well. Stir in the beaten eggs, add the melted butter and beat mixture vigorously for 2 minutes. Bake about 20 minutes in a hot oven (400° F.) in well-buttered muffin pans.

Crackling Bread

1 cup cracklings (diced)
1½ cups corn meal
¾ cup wheat flour
½ teaspoon soda
¼ teaspoon salt
1 cup sour milk

Cracklings are the pieces of meat remaining after the lard has been rendered from the pork. Mix and sift together the dry ingredients. Add the milk, stir in the cracklings. Form into oblong cakes and place in greased baking pan. Bake in hot oven (400° F.) 30 minutes.

Louisiana Waffles

2 cups flour
4 teaspoons baking powder
½ teaspoon salt
5 tablespoons melted butter
1½ cups milk
3 eggs

To beaten yolks add milk, and all other ingredients with the exception of stiffly-beaten whites of eggs which are to be added last. Pour a spoonful of batter in each section of a hot waffle iron and bake until rich golden brown.

Virginia Waffles

1½ cups boiling water
½ cup white corn meal
1½ cups milk
3 cups flour
3 tablespoons sugar
3 teaspoons baking powder
½ teaspoon salt
2 eggs
3 tablespoons melted butter

Cook the meal in the boiling water 30 minutes; add milk, dry ingredients, well-beaten egg yolks, butter, and well-beaten egg whites. Put one tablespoon of waffle mixture in each compartment near the center. Cook on greased hot waffle iron or ungreased electric waffle iron until well puffed and a delicate brown.

Georgia Flapjacks

2 cups flour
1½ teaspoons baking soda
½ teaspoon salt
1 tablespoon sugar
2 eggs
2 cups sour milk
1¼ tablespoons melted butter

Sift the flour and measure two cupfuls. Sift again. Add soda, salt and sugar, mix well and sift once more. Beat eggs lightly, add milk and gradually add these ingredients to the flour mixture. Beat until smooth and free from lumps and then add the butter. Pour the batter into a pitcher. Heat a griddle or a heavy frying pan and butter it. Pour enough batter on to the pan to make a cake about five inches in diameter. Cook until porous and brown underneath and then brown on the other side.

Rice Waffles

1 cup cooked rice
2 cups flour
2 eggs
1 teaspoon salt
3 teaspoons baking powder
2 tablespoons melted butter
a little milk

After beating yolks of eggs, add rice, butter, flour, baking powder and salt, and then the well-beaten whites of eggs. A little milk may be added if necessary. Cook on greased hot waffle iron or ungreased electric waffle iron.

Sour Milk Griddle Cakes

1½ cups flour
1 cup sour milk or buttermilk
1 tablespoon melted butter
½ teaspoon salt
1 teaspoon baking soda
1 tablespoon sugar
2 eggs

Sift the flour and sugar; dissolve the soda in the buttermilk and add to the flour. Drop in the unbeaten eggs, beat well and lastly add the melted butter. Drop by spoonful on a hot greased griddle and brown on both sides.

Flannel Cakes

2 eggs
1½ cups milk
2 cups flour
½ teaspoon salt
2 teaspoons sugar
2 tablespoons melted butter
3 teaspoons baking powder

Sift baking powder, salt, sugar and flour. Beat the egg yolks well and add to the milk. Pour this into the flour, add the melted butter and lastly the well beaten egg whites. Drop by spoonful on a hot greased griddle, brown on both sides and serve hot with syrup. Pork sausage goes well with flannel cakes.

Griddle Cakes

2 cups flour
2 eggs
2 teaspoons baking powder
½ teaspoon salt
2 tablespoons melted butter
1 heaping tablespoon sugar
1½ cups milk

Sift flour, salt, sugar and baking powder, add the milk and egg yolks, beat well and then add the melted butter. Beat the egg whites to a stiff froth and add last. Bake on a hot griddle greased lightly.

I love my wife, I love my baby,
I love dem flapjacks flopped in gravy.
Mourners, you shall be free, you shall be free,
When de good Lord sets you free.

Beaten Biscuits

3 cups sifted flour
½ cup milk
⅓ cup lard
½ teaspoon salt
¾ teaspoon sugar

Sift sugar and salt into the flour, blend in the lard and make a very stiff dough, using more or less of the milk as needed as the dough must be stiff. Place on a floured board and roll until it blisters and is smooth. Roll to ½ inch in thickness, cut with biscuit cutter, stick with a fork and bake in a moderate oven (350° F.) for half an hour.

Mammy's Baking Powder Biscuits

2 cups flour
4 teaspoons baking powder
¼ teaspoon salt
2 tablespoons shortening
½ cup milk

Sift dry ingredients together. Work in shortening with finger tips. Then add milk slowly, stirring the batter until it is smooth. Roll the dough on a floured board until it is ½ inch thick. Cut with a cookie cutter and bake in a hot (450° F.) oven for fifteen minutes.

Good Morning Biscuits

1 tablespoon butter
1 egg, well beaten
1 tablespoon sugar
1 teaspoon lard
1 pint of milk
1 heaping teaspoon salt
½ yeast cake dissolved in
¼ cup lukewarm water
6 cups flour

Pour milk, butter, salt, lard, and sugar into a double boiler and scald; let mixture cool until lukewarm; then dissolve yeast and stir into the mixture. When mixture has cooled, add 2½ cups of flour and mix into a stiff batter. Then add one well-beaten egg to the batter and put in a warm place to rise. After about five hours, knead as for biscuits using the balance of the flour, and when the dough can be handled easily roll out to ½ inch thickness. Cut with a biscuit cutter, butter the tops of biscuits, placing one on top of the other to form a double biscuit, and place in pan far enough apart so that they will not touch each other. Bake for about ¼ of an hour in a hot oven (400° F.).

Corn Sticks

2 cups corn meal
1 cup milk
1 egg
1 tablespoon lard
2 teaspoons baking powder
½ teaspoon salt

Beat all together and bake in greased tins the shape of bread sticks or ears of corn in a quick oven (500° F.) for 10 to 12 minutes.

Raisin Biscuits

2½ cups flour
2 eggs
⅓ cup butter
¾ cup milk
4 teaspoons baking powder
½ teaspoon salt
1 tablespoon sugar
1½ cups seeded raisins

Sift flour, sugar, baking powder and salt Beat the eggs and. add to the milk. Mix the shortening into the flour, stir in the milk and egg. Add the raisins. Turn onto a well-floured board and knead until smooth, using more flour if necessary. Cut with small biscuit cutter and bake in a hot oven (450° F.) for 15 minutes. Serve hot.

Buttermilk Muffins

1 quart buttermilk
2 eggs
1 tablespoon sugar
4 cups sifted flour
2 tablespoons corn meal
1 teaspoon salt
1 teaspoon soda

Cream sugar and eggs, add milk and finally the flour, corn meal, salt and soda, which has been sifted three times. Beat hard one minute and bake in a hot oven (400° F.) for 20 minutes in greased muffin tins.

Cheese Biscuits

½ cup flour
¼ pound grated cheese
¼ pound butter
salt to taste
3 tablespoons ice water

Mix quickly with as little handling as possible. Roll thin, cut with cookie cutter and bake in a quick oven (500° F.) for 10 minutes.

Batter Bread, Mulatto Style

1 egg
½ cup cold hominy
1 teaspoon salt
½ pint corn meal
1 tablespoon lard

Mix the cold hominy, beaten egg, corn meal and salt with enough boiling water to make a batter of the consistency of milk. Put the lard in a deep baking pan and heat until it smokes. Pour into this hot lard the cold batter; the melted lard will bubble up on the side of the pan, making a delicious crust. Bake in a moderate oven (350° F.) about forty minutes.

Creole Rice Cakes

4 slices bacon, chopped
3 tablespoons chopped onion
3 tablespoons green pepper
1 teaspoon salt
½ teaspoon pepper
3 cups rice, cooked
1 cup flour
1 teaspoon baking powder
1 can tomato pulp

Fry the bacon crisp leaving the bacon fat in frying pan. Chop bacon and add to onion, pepper and rest of ingredients. Mix thoroughly. Fry in the bacon fat as pancakes.

Dinah's Rice Croquettes

2½ cups cooked rice
1 cup grated American cheese
½ cup butter or other shortening
½ cup chopped pimento
1 tablespoon chopped onion
⅛ teaspoon salt and paprika
1 teaspoon baking powder
1 egg beaten well
½ cup buttered bread crumbs

Mix all well and mold into balls and fry in hot fat until brown.

Baked Hominy or Grits

1 cup cold boiled hominy
½ cup milk
1 egg
1 tablespoon butter
½ teaspoon salt
1 pinch pepper

Heat the milk and butter, add the hominy and mix until smooth. Then add the beaten egg, seasoning and pour into a buttered baking dish and bake slowly in a moderate oven (350° F.) until firm and brown.

Mulatto Rice

½ pound bacon
1 small onion
1 cup tomatoes
2 cups cooked rice

Cut the bacon in small pieces and fry. Remove from the skillet and brown the minced onion in the bacon fat. Add the tomatoes and cooked rice. Blend well and serve.

Curried Rice

2 cups cooked rice
1 diced green pepper
1 diced onion
2 cups tomatoes
3 cups water
4 tablespoons butter
1½ teaspoons curry powder

Mix all the ingredients. Put in a well greased casserole and bake in a slow oven until the onions and peppers are well cooked.

Wild Rice and Mushrooms

1 cup wild rice
3 cups boiling water
1 pound fresh mushrooms
2 tablespoons butter
2 tablespoons flour
1 cup milk
salt to taste

Cover the rice with boiling water and let boil fast for 15 minutes, or until water is well absorbed; then let steam until it is dry and fluffy. Peel the mushrooms, sauté in the butter until well browned. Remove mushrooms from the skillet and add the flour to the butter, rubbing to a smooth paste. Then add the milk and cook until thick. Add the mushrooms to this and heat. Pour mushrooms over rice and serve.

Rice and Pineapple

1 large sized can sliced pineapple
4 cups cooked rice
1 cup brown sugar

Put ½ inch layer of cooked rice in the bottom of a casserole, then dot with butter and place the pineapple over the top. Sprinkle with some of the brown sugar. Repeat this until all the rice is used, having the top layer of pineapple. Pour the juice from the can over this and bake in a moderate oven (350° F.) for 30 minutes.

Rice Flour Waffles

1 cup cooked cold hominy
2 eggs
1 cup rice flour
⅓ cup wheat flour
¼ teaspoon salt
1 cup milk
⅛ cup water
2 tablespoons melted butter

Beat the cold hominy into the egg until it is smooth. Mix and sift the dry ingredients, then add the milk and water and mix to a batter. Then add the egg and hominy mixture and last the melted butter. Bake in a hot waffle iron a little longer than is usual for plain waffles. Serve piping hot with lots of butter.

Two little niggers lyin' in bed,
One of 'em sick an' de odder mos' dead.
Call for de doctor, an' de doctor said,
"Feed dem darkies on short'nin' bread."

Hashed Browned Potatoes

1 pound salt pork
⅓ cup fat
2 cups cold boiled potatoes
⅛ teaspoon pepper
salt (if necessary)

Fry fat out of salt pork; cut in cubes and remove scraps. (There should be ⅓ cup of fat.) Mix the boiled potatoes thoroughly with the fat; add pepper and salt; fry three minutes, stirring constantly. Let stand, to brown underneath, and fry as you would an omelet.

Candied Yams

Parboil sweet potatoes or yams, and pare and cut in halves, lengthwise in a casserole, sprinkling each layer as it is set in place, with salt, paprika, brown sugar. Dot with bits of butter and add a few dashes of cinnamon. Pour in about half a cupful of boiling water, cover and bake until tender. When about half baked, lift the potatoes on the bottom of the dish placing them on the top of the dish. Add more water if necessary.

Stuffed Sweet Potatoes

6 sweet potatoes
2 tablespoons butter
table cream to moisten
½ teaspoon salt

Bake the potatoes, scoop out the centers and add the salt, butter and cream to soften. Refill the skins and bake in a hot oven for about five minutes.

Piedmont Potato Croquettes

2 cups hot riced potatoes
2 tablespoons butter
1 whole egg
3 egg yolks
1 cup sifted flour
½ cup finely-chopped blanched almonds
½ teaspoon salt
1 pinch paprika

Mix the potatoes, butter, egg yolks, salt and pepper and beat thoroughly. Shape in balls using one tablespoon of the mixture for each ball. Roll in flour and dip in the beaten egg and then roll in the almonds. Fry in deep hot fat (390° F.) until golden brown, which usually requires about one minute.

Corn Meal Mush

1 cup corn meal
2 quarts boiling water
1 teaspoon salt

Moisten corn meal with enough cold water to make a paste. Stir paste into boiling salted water, beating thoroughly. Let cook over slow fire stirring almost constantly for 1 hour. Put in double boiler and cook 3 hours longer. Serve hot with sugar and cream. To fry: Pack hot into well-greased baking pan and let stand until cold and solid. Cut in ½-inch strips, roll in flour and fry on buttered griddle until brown on both sides. Serve with syrup and sausage.

Yam Puff

4 large yams or sweet potatoes
¼ cup butter
2 well-beaten eggs
⅓ cup sugar
2 teaspoons baking powder
1 teaspoon salt

Peel potatoes and boil until soft. Mash and add the remaining ingredients. Beat well and put in buttered casserole. Dot with butter and bake until brown, about ½ hour or more.

Georgian Style Sweet Potatoes

3 cups mashed sweet potato
2 tablespoons molasses
1 tablespoon butter

Mash the sweet potatoes and place in a buttered casserole. Boil together the molasses and butter for 7 minutes. Pour over the sweet potatoes and bake in a moderate oven until delicately brown.

Sweet Potato Pone

2 cups grated sweet potato
1 cup butter
1 cup sugar
½ cup milk
1 teaspoon powdered ginger
grated rind of one orange

Blend the sugar and butter, add grated sweet potato and milk; beat well and then add the ginger and orange rind. Place in a shallow baking pan and bake in a slow oven.

Baked Stuffed Potatoes

Bake large potatoes, cut in halves lengthwise, and scoop out the center. Mix this with 1 teaspoon salt, 2 tablespoons butter, enough cream or milk to soften, and one egg. Beat well, return to potato shells and brown on top. Sprinkle with paprika before serving.

Scalloped Potatoes

Slice about 6 raw potatoes with a slaw cutter. Cover the bottom of a baking dish with bread crumbs, bits of butter and a little parsley. Put over it a layer of potatoes, salt and pepper. Alternate potatoes and bread crumbs until dish is full. Pour a cup of milk over it and bake in moderate oven (350° F.) for one hour.

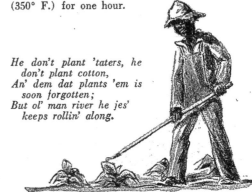

*He don't plant 'taters, he
   don't plant cotton,
An' dem dat plants 'em is
   soon forgotten;
But ol' man river he jes'
   keeps rollin' along.*

Sugared Yams

2 cups water
2 cups sugar
2 tablespoons butter
    dash nutmeg
8 uncooked yams

Bring the sugar and water to a boil and add the butter and nutmeg. Peel and slice the yams, drop into boiling syrup, cover and cook slowly until yams are done and transparent.

Pineapple Marshmallow Sweet Potatoes

(I'll have it with my Roast . . . and again for Dessert)

2 cups mashed sweet potatoes
1 cup milk
½ cup pineapple juice
1 cup diced pineapple
2 tablespoons butter
½ teaspoon cinnamon
    marshmallows

Thoroughly mix all the ingredients and beat until light and fluffy. Use more milk or fruit juice, if needed. Place in buttered casserole and bake until heated through. Remove from oven and cover the top with marshmallows. Return to oven to brown. Serve with poultry or roast.

Strawberry Jam Cake

1 cup butter
½ cup sugar
1 cup strawberry jam
½ cup strong black coffee
1 teaspoon cinnamon
¼ teaspoon cloves
3 eggs, separated
2½ cups flour
1 teaspoon soda, dissolved in
4 tablespoons sour cream

Cream butter well, add sugar gradually and beat well. Add jam and coffee to which spices have been added. Beat yolks of eggs and blend with first mixture. Sift flour and add alternately with sour cream in which soda has been dissolved. Fold in the stiffly beaten egg whites. Bake in layers in moderate oven (350° F.) 45 to 55 minutes. Ice with favorite icing.

Scalloped Sweet Potatoes

Peel and dice six sweet potatoes. Drop them in boiling water and allow them to parboil about 15 minutes. Drain the potatoes, dust with salt, add one tablespoonful butter and ⅓ pint cream and finish baking them in a moderate oven until brown.

Sweet Potatoes in Honey

(Easy to Make—Delicious)

Peel six sweet potatoes. Cut them in ¼-inch slices lengthwise. Boil them fifteen minutes. Drain and remove to warm casserole. Add a small jar of honey, the juice of an orange, salt. Finish by baking in the oven.

Blackberry Roll

2 quarts blackberries
1 pint flour
2 cups sugar
2 tablespoons butter
    ice water
¼ teaspoon salt

First, mix flour and salt into which cut two tablespoons butter. After mixing well add enough ice water to make a stiff dough. Clean berries thoroughly and set them to soak with two cups of sugar. Roll dough very thin (on floured board) into an oblong sheet. Pour berries on one end of pastry dough, roll over and pour more berries, roll again and so on until berries are all used. Place in buttered baking pan. Bake in a moderate oven (350° F.) about thirty to thirty-five minutes. When the roll has baked this length of time begin basting with the following mixture every five minutes for another half hour:

1 tablespoon butter—melted
½ cup sugar

Serve with powdered sugar or favorite sauce in dish in which it has been baked.

Pecan Nut Cake

3 cups nutmeats, finely chopped
6 eggs
1 tablespoon flour
1½ cups sugar
1 teaspoon baking powder
½ teaspoon salt
1 teaspoon vanilla
    boiled orange icing

Beat the egg yolks until very light, add the sugar gradually and beat well. Sift together the flour, baking powder and salt; add the nuts and then combine with egg mixture. Beat well. Stir in the stiffly beaten egg whites and vanilla and bake in two layer cake tins in a moderate oven (350° F.) from 30 to 40 minutes. When cool ice with "Boiled Orange Icing" (see page 44) and cover top with whole pecans. Whipped cream may be substituted for icing on top.

Peas in the pot, hoecake a bakin',
Sally in de kitchen with her shirt-tail a-shakin'.

Pie Dough or Southern Pastry

2 cups flour
½ teaspoon salt
1 cup butter or other shortening
½ cup ice water

Mix flour and salt, work butter lightly into the flour, add ice water and mix to make a stiff dough but do not knead. Roll and line pie plate.

Chess Pie

½ cup butter
1 cup sugar
   yolks of 3 eggs
   white of 1 egg
1 cup chopped raisins
1 cup chopped nut meats
1 teaspoon vanilla

Cream butter and sugar, add the beaten yolks of 3 eggs and stiffly-beaten white of 1 egg. Stir until it foams. Add the fruit and nuts and put in patty shells and bake in hot oven (400° F.) until fillings set and then in a moderate oven (350° F.) until well browned. Serve with whipped cream. This recipe makes 12 individual pies.

Kentucky Pie

(From the Idle Hour Farm)

3 cups brown sugar
3 eggs
½ cup butter
½ cup cream
1 teaspoon vanilla
1 pinch salt

Cream the butter, eggs and sugar together and then add the balance of the ingredients. Fill a pie shell and bake in a moderate oven (350° F.) 30 minutes.

Real Southern Lemon Pie

1½ cups sugar
⅓ cup pastry flour
3 eggs, separated
1¼ cups water
   pinch of salt
1 tablespoon butter
1 lemon (juice)
   grated rind of one lemon

Place in double boiler the sugar and 1 cup of water, to it add the butter and salt. Blend the flour with the remaining ¼ cup of water and add to the sugar and water. Then gradually add the beaten egg yolks and let cook until it thickens, remove from the fire and let cool, then add the lemon juice and rind. Put in baked pie shell and place on top the well beaten egg whites to which 2 tablespoons of confectioners sugar have been added and well beaten. Bake in slow oven (300° F.) until the meringue browns.

Beef steaks, poke chop,
Gimme a little sop,
Make a nigger's mouth go flippity flop.

Jelly Pie

1 unbaked pie shell
4 egg whites, well beaten
4 egg yolks, well beaten
½ cup strawberry jelly
½ cup butter
1½ cups sugar
1 teaspoon lemon juice

Cream butter, adding sugar slowly and beat well. Add yolks and jelly and fold in the whites of eggs. Mix in the lemon juice and pour in pie shell. Bake in a moderate oven (350° F.) for about thirty minutes.

Cocoanut Pie

½ cup shredded cocoanut
3 eggs, separated
½ cup sugar
2 cups scalded milk
   pinch of salt

Beat yolks with sugar and pinch of salt. Add well beaten whites. Stir in scalded milk and last mix in the cocoanut. Bake in a deep pie plate with under crust only, hot oven (475° F.) for first 15 minutes and moderate oven (350° F.) for half hour.

Pumpkin Pie

1 cup canned or baked and strained pumpkin
¼ cup sugar
½ teaspoon salt
¼ teaspoon mace
¼ teaspoon cinnamon
½ teaspoon vanilla
½ teaspoon cloves
¼ teaspoon ginger
2 beaten eggs
½ cup milk
½ cup cream

Mix dry ingredients. Add pumpkin, eggs, milk and cream gradually. Bake for 15 minutes in a hot (475° F.) oven and for 25 minutes in a moderate oven (350° F.), in a pie plate lined with plain pastry for pie crusts.

(To bake pumpkin for pie, wash and cut the pumpkin in half crosswise. Scrape out seeds and stringy parts. Place in dripping pan, shell side up, and bake until it begins to fall apart and is tender. Scrape pulp from shell and strain.)

White House Pecan Pie

1 cup unbroken pecan meats
1 cup dark table syrup
2 tablespoons butter
2 eggs
1 cup sugar
1 teaspoon vanilla

Cream the butter and sugar, add the table syrup, the beaten eggs, the pecans and vanilla. Beat together well. Put in unbaked pie shell and bake in a slow oven (275° F.) for about 30 minutes. Serve with whipped cream.

Apple Pot Pie

½ dozen baking apples
½ cup butter or other shortening
4 cups flour
¼ teaspoon salt
¼ teaspoon cinnamon
⅛ pound butter

Make a dough of flour, shortening, and salt, add sufficient water to form dough. Roll thin on a floured board and cut in two-inch squares. Pare and core apples and cut into small pieces. Place apples in a kettle and sprinkle liberally with sugar and cinnamon. Alternate layers of dough and apples. Place butter on top, fill kettle half full of water, cover, and cook until apples are done. Serve with fresh milk or cream.

Carrot Pudding

2 tablespoons butter
1 cup sugar
2 eggs
1½ cups grated raw carrots
¼ teaspoon ground cloves
½ teaspoon cinnamon
¼ teaspoon nutmeg
¼ teaspoon salt
1 cup flour, sifted
   grated rind of 1 orange
   grated rind of 1 lemon
1 teaspoon soda
1 cup grated raw potatoes
¼ pound thinly sliced citron

Cream the butter and sugar; add eggs and beat well. Add carrots, spices and salt, sifted flour, orange and lemon rinds to the mixture. Add the soda to the grated raw potatoes and stir until it is dissolved; add potatoes to carrot

and flour mixture. Add citron, mixing it well through the batter. Butter a mold and place a sheet of greased paper on the bottom; pour in the pudding. Cover the mold and place it in a pot of boiling water to steam for 2 hours. The pudding may be served with cream or your favorite sauce.

Raisin Pie

1 cup seeded raisins, washed
2 cups water
1½ cups sugar
4 tablespoons flour
1 egg, well beaten
   juice of a lemon
2 teaspoons grated lemon rind
1 pinch of salt

Soak raisins 3 hours. Mix sugar, flour and egg, then add seasoning, raisins and liquid. Cook over hot water for 15 minutes, stirring occasionally. When the mixture is cool, empty into pie dough lined pie- plate. Cover pie with narrow strips of dough criss-crossed, bake in a hot oven (450° F.) for 20 minutes and in a moderate oven (350° F.) for 10 minutes.

Butterscotch Pie

1 cup brown sugar
2 tablespoons butter
2 generous teaspoons flour
1 egg yolk
1 cup milk
1 egg white beaten well

Boil the sugar and butter together until soft. Beat the egg yolk well and add it to the flour, then adding the milk. Beat this until very smooth. Mix this well into the sugar and butter, and cook until it thickens. Lemon or vanilla can be used for flavoring. Pour this into a pie pan lined with the baked pie crust. To the beaten egg white add 1 tablespoon sugar, spread over top of pie and brown in oven.

Nannie's Pineapple Custard Pie

¾ cup sugar
1 cup grated pineapple, from which juice has been strained
1 cup milk
2 tablespoons corn starch
3 eggs

Mix the corn starch, sugar and milk together and put in double boiler. Separate the eggs and place the yolks in with the sugar and milk. Cook until thick. Remove from over the hot water and add the pineapple and the beaten egg whites. Put in baked pie shell and when cool cover with unsweetened whipped cream.

Ambrosia

6 oranges
1½ cups sugar
1½ cups freshly grated cocoanut
   sherry wine

Peel and divide oranges into sections, arrange pieces on bottom of glass dish and sprinkle generously with sugar and cocoanut, repeat until ingredients are used. Pour over about a wineglass sherry wine. Chill in ice box.

Plum Pudding

(Christmas "Ain't" Christmas Without Plum Puddin')

1 cup suet, chopped fine
1 cup cooking molasses
1 cup seedless raisins
1 cup chopped dates
1 cup chopped apples
1 cup currants
1 cup chopped walnut meats
½ cup sugar
2 cups milk
1 teaspoon soda
1 teaspoon baking powder
½ teaspoon cinnamon
½ teaspoon cloves
½ teaspoon salt
1 egg
flour enough to make a stiff batter

Mix all the ingredients and pour into a covered mold ¾ full. Place mold on trivet in kettle containing boiling water. The water should come half way up around the mold. Keep water at boiling point for 3 hours. Serve with brandied hard sauce.

Orange Marmalade Bread Pudding

2 cups stale bread crumbs
2 cups scalded milk
½ cup sugar
2 tablespoons melted butter
3 eggs, slightly beaten
2 teaspoons vanilla
1 glass orange marmalade
1 teaspoon nutmeg

Soak the bread crumbs in the milk; when cool add the sugar, butter, eggs, flavoring and marmalade. Place in a buttered baking dish and bake in a slow oven (250° F.) 1 hour.

Queen of Trifles Pudding

½ pound lady fingers
8 macaroons
¼ pound blanched almonds
¼ pound crystallized fruit
3 cups boiled custard
1 cup whipped cream
½ cup sherry

Break the lady fingers and macaroons into small coarse pieces and cover with the sherry, add the chopped nuts and the fruit cut in small pieces. Mix together and pour the boiled custard over all. When ready to serve top with the sweetened whipped cream.

Boiled Custard

1½ cups milk
1 tablespoon sugar
1 teaspoon vanilla
2 eggs

Beat eggs slightly and add the sugar and mix. Slowly add the scalded milk and pour all into the top of a double boiler and cook until the mixture coats the spoon (about 10 minutes). Remove from fire and add flavoring.

Apple Dumpling

2 cups flour
4 teaspoons baking powder
1 teaspoon salt
4 tablespoons shortening
1 cup milk
6 apples, pared and cored
sugar and cinnamon

Sift flour, baking powder and salt; cut in shortening, add milk and mix to smooth dough. Turn onto floured board and divide into six portions. Roll each large enough to cover one apple. Place apple on each piece of dough . . . fill with cinnamon and sugar . . . wet edges of dough and fold over apple . . . Place on greased baking pan, and bake in moderate oven (350° F.) until apples are tender (about ½ hour).

Monticello Pandowdy

6 apples
1½ cups molasses
1 teaspoon nutmeg
2 teaspoons cinnamon
½ teaspoon ground cloves
pie crust

Pare and core the apples and cut in small pieces. Cover with cold water and let stand for 10 minutes. Remove apples from water and drain. Into a buttered baking dish place the apples and cover with the molasses and spices. Cover the top with a pie crust and bake in moderate oven (350° F.) until done, about 1 hour. When cold, break the crust into the apple mixture and place on the fire to simmer for a few minutes. When well cooled serve with cream.

Southern Batter Pudding

3 eggs
2 tablespoons sugar
¼ cup flour
¾ cup milk
1 teaspoon melted butter
½ teaspoon vanilla
¼ teaspoon salt

Add sugar to well-beaten egg yolks and beat again. Mix butter, salt and vanilla into above and add flour and milk alternately. Lastly fold in the stiffly-beaten egg whites. Pour into a well-buttered mold. Place mold in pan of water and steam about one hour or until firm; serve pudding hot with chocolate or favorite pudding sauce.

*There was a little
Alabamy coon
An' he ain't been
born very long;*

* * *

*Oh dey took him
down to the cot-
ton fields
An' he rolled an'
he tumbled in de
sun!*

Plantation Plum Pudding

1 cup suet, chopped fine
4 eggs
1 cup toasted bread crumbs
1 cup chopped citron
1 cup chopped pecans
1 cup chopped blanched almonds
2 cups finely chopped apples
2 cups seeded raisins
½ cup currants
½ cup sugar
1 teaspoon cinnamon
½ teaspoon allspice
1 lemon, juice and grated rind
½ cup brandy
½ teaspoon grated nutmeg
1 teaspoon cloves

Beat whole eggs and slowly add the other ingredients, being very careful that they are well mixed. Place in a covered mold ¾ full and steam in a large steamer for about 3 hours. To steam, the mold is placed on a trivet in a kettle containing boiling water which comes half way up around the mold. Serve with a brandied hard sauce. (See page 24.)

Molasses Pudding

1 egg
2 tablespoons sugar
½ cup molasses
2 tablespoons melted butter
1½ cups flour
½ cup boiling water
1 pinch salt
1 teaspoon baking soda dissolved in hot water

Beat the egg and sugar, add the butter, water, soda, and molasses and then beat in the flour and a little salt. Put in a double boiler and let steam for one hour. Serve with foaming pudding sauce. (See page 24.)

Bread Pudding

4 slices buttered bread cut in squares
½ cup sugar
3 eggs
vanilla
½ pint rich milk

Beat eggs and sugar, add milk and vanilla, add buttered bread and bake in slow oven (300° F.) for about 40 minutes or until custard is done.

*Carry me back to old Virginny,
There's where the cotton and the corn and tatoes grow;
There's where the birds warble, sweet in the springtime,
There's where the old darkey's heart am long'd to go.*

Barbara Fritchie Pudding

¾ cup granulated sugar
½ cup whipping cream
¾ cup brown sugar
2 egg yolks
2 egg whites
2 tablespoons butter
nutmeg
½ teaspoon vanilla

Into a double boiler put the sugar, cream, brown sugar, egg yolks and butter and cook until thick. Remove from the fire, add the vanilla and the well-beaten egg whites. Pour into unbaked pie shell, sprinkle with nutmeg, bake in a slow oven (275° F.) for about 45 minutes or until custard is set. Serve very cold.

Rice Custard

½ cup brown sugar
2 cups cooked rice
3 tablespoons butter
1 cup milk
3 eggs
½ cup raisins
½ teaspoon vanilla
dash of nutmeg

To the rice add the sugar, butter, milk and slightly beaten eggs. Place in deep dish and bake in moderate oven (350° F.) for 1 hour. When half done remove from oven and add the raisins and vanilla, and sprinkle with nutmeg. Replace in oven and continue baking.

Paulina's Delicious Cottage Pudding
(Second Helpin's, Please)

2 cups sifted cake flour
2 teaspoons baking powder
½ teaspoon salt
3 tablespoons butter
1 cup sugar
1 cup milk
½ teaspoon vanilla

Sift flour once. After measuring, add baking powder and salt, and then sift again. Cream butter, add sugar gradually, and cream together well. Add the flour, alternately with milk, a small amount at a time, beating after each addition until smooth. Add vanilla. Bake in greased pan, 8x8x2 inches, in moderate oven (350° F.) about one hour. Serve hot with chocolate or lemon sauce.

Orange Cake

5 eggs
1¼ cups sugar
1¼ cups flour
juice of ½ orange
1 teaspoon baking powder

Beat well the yolks of eggs, add sugar and beat until smooth. Add the orange juice, mix well. Add flour and baking powder that have been sifted together. When thoroughly mixed fold in the stiffly beaten egg whites and bake in 2 layers in a moderate oven (350° F.) for 40 minutes. Put together with the orange filling.

Miss Rosa's Gingerbread

1 cup molasses
1 cup brown sugar
½ cup melted butter
2 eggs
1 teaspoon cinnamon
1 teaspoon ginger
1 teaspoon cloves
1 teaspoon baking soda
1 cup boiling water
3 cups flour

Stir brown sugar into melted butter and add the unbeaten eggs. Beat well. Dissolve baking soda in the boiling water and add the spices. Beat well and add the flour. Pour into a large pan (8 x 8) and bake in a moderate oven (350° F.) until thoroughly baked, about 25 minutes.

None-So-Good Jelly Roll

5 eggs, separated
1 cup sugar
1 cup flour
    grated rind of 1 lemon
2 tablespoons lemon juice

Beat yolks well and add sugar; beat until thick, add lemon rind and juice and half of the flour and half of the stiffly-beaten whites, then the rest of the eggs and flour. Pour into large, well-greased pan, not more than ¼ inch thick. Bake in a moderate oven (375° F.) between 10 and 15 minutes. Turn on sheet of heavy paper or damp cloth. Beat jelly with fork and spread, on cake. Trim off crusty edges and roll while warm. Wrap in paper or cloth and set aside to cool.

Crêpes Suzette New Orleans

2 eggs
1½ cups milk
    grated rind of ½ lemon
¼ teaspoon salt
1 cup cake flour
1 tablespoon powdered sugar
1 wineglass champagne, white wine or
    brandy
12 lumps sugar
1 orange, juice and grated rind
½ cup melted butter

Beat the eggs until light and lemon-colored; gradually stir in the milk, lemon rind and salt. Sift the powdered sugar with the flour and slowly beat the milk mixture into the flour. Drop batter by large tablespoonfuls on hot greased griddle. The batter should be thin enough to spread very easily. Fry slowly on one side; turn and fry until other side is golden brown. Make Suzette sauce as follows: Pour a wineglass of champagne, white wine or brandy into a chafing dish. Crush the lumps of sugar in the orange juice and add to the champagne which has been heating in the chafing dish. Add a little of the grated orange rind and ½ cup melted butter. Cover and cook until a thick smooth sauce results. Dip each pancake as it is prepared into sauce; lift it out and roll it; sprinkle with powdered sugar and serve immediately.

Old-Fashioned Strawberry Shortcake

2 cups flour
4 teaspoons baking powder
1 pinch salt
2 large tablespoons butter
½ cup milk

Add salt and baking powder to flour and lightly blend the butter into the flour, adding milk last. Place on floured board and pat into two large cakes. Place one upon the other and bake in a hot (450° F.) oven for 15 or 20 minutes. Crush strawberries and sweeten. Cut cake in about six equal sections as you would a pie, break each section horizontally in half and spread the center liberally with butter and crushed berries. Replace top and cover with berries. Whipped cream may be added if desired.

Other fruits such as peaches or raspberries may be substituted for strawberries.

Hot Frosted Gingerbread

½ cup butter
½ cup strong hot coffee
2 eggs
½ cup sugar
½ cup molasses
2 teaspoons baking powder
1 teaspoon ginger
1½ cups flour

Melt the butter with the hot coffee. Beat the eggs and stir in the sugar and molasses. Combine this with the warm mixture. Sift in flour and ginger to make a soft drop batter. Stir in the baking powder, and spread the batter ½ inch thick on a greased and floured dripping pan. Bake 25 minutes in a moderate (350° F.) oven. While hot frost this with one cupful of confectioner's sugar, stirred with four tablespoons of cream. Flavor with vanilla.

Raw Apple Float

3 apples
4 tablespoons sugar
5 egg whites
    nutmeg

Peel and grate the apples and then drain off liquid. Beat the whites of eggs stiff and gradually add the sugar. Fold in the grated apple slowly, beating all the time. Pour into a serving bowl and sprinkle top with nutmeg. Place in ice box until very cold and serve.

Ah love me a frin'less woman,
An' her name is Julie Anne.
She treats me like a dirty dog,
But ah do's de best ah can.

Bride's Angel Food Cake

whites of 18 eggs
1 pound sugar
1 pound sifted flour
¾ pound butter
1 teaspoon baking soda
2 teaspoons cream of tartar
1 teaspoon vanilla

Sift flour three times, and add soda and cream of tartar, then cream butter and sugar until very light and add to the stiffly-beaten whites of eggs gradually. Add the flour beating it lightly, flavor with teaspoon of vanilla. Place in angel food pan and bake in a slow oven (250° F.).

Fruit Cake

2 cups blanched almonds
3 cups seeded raisins
2 cups currants
2 cups crystallized cherries
2 cups chopped dried figs
2 cups chopped dates
1 cup chopped citron
2 cups crystallized pineapple
1 cup chopped lemon peel
1 cup chopped orange peel
3 cups light brown sugar
3 cups butter
3 cups flour
12 eggs, separated
1 wineglass brandy
2 tablespoons cinnamon
2 tablespoons mace
2 tablespoons cloves
2 tablespoons allspice
2 tablespoons nutmeg
1 tablespoon soda in a little water

Cream sugar and butter, add the well-beaten egg yolks. Then gradually add a little of each fruit which has been well dredged in some of the flour. Put in the spices, brandy and the remaining flour. Beat the egg whites to a stiff froth and add. Dissolve the baking soda in a little warm water and add last. Bake in a deep pan, in a slow oven 2½ to 3 hours, or until done when tried with a toothpick.

Lady Baltimore Cake

2 cups confectioner's sugar
1 cup butter
3 cups flour
3 teaspoons baking powder
½ teaspoon salt
1 cup milk
6 egg whites

Cream the butter and sugar together. Sift the baking powder and flour together twice, add the salt and mix with the butter and sugar and the milk. Beat thoroughly. Beat the whites of eggs until stiff and add. Stir well and bake in buttered layer-cake pans for twenty minutes in a moderate (375° F.) oven. Spread the layers with a favorite icing.

Plantation Marble Cake

2 cups sifted cake flour
2 teaspoons baking powder
¼ teaspoon salt
½ cup butter or other shortening
1 cup sugar
2 eggs, well beaten
⅔ cup milk
1 teaspoon cinnamon
½ teaspoon cloves
½ teaspoon nutmeg
2 tablespoons molasses

Sift flour once. After measuring, add baking powder and salt, and sift together three times. Cream the butter thoroughly, add the sugar gradually, and cream together until light and fluffy. Add the eggs; then flour, alternately with milk, a small amount at a time. Beat after each addition until smooth. Divide the batter into two parts. To the one part, add spices and molasses. Drop by tablespoons into greased loaf pan, alternating light and dark mixtures. Bake in moderate oven (350° F.) one hour and fifteen minutes, or until done. Spread butter frosting on top and sides of cake.

Palm Beach Poincianna Cake

(Dainty, Delectable, Delicious)

1 pound sugar
1 pound flour (3¼ cups)
1 pound butter
juice and rind of one lemon
9 eggs, separated
2 cups chopped blanched almonds
½ pound citron, chopped fine
½ pound raisins, chopped fine

Cream butter and sugar and add to well-beaten yolks of eggs. Then add alternately the flour and the whites beaten stiff; dredge the fruits and nuts with flour and add to the batter. Bake in layer tins in a slow oven (300° F.) from 40 to 50 minutes.

Poincianna Cake Filling

2 cups sugar
1 cup boiling water
juice and grated rind of two lemons
1 tablespoon corn starch
2 cups grated cocoanut

Boil the first three ingredients and add the corn starch, which you have dissolved in a little cold water. Cook until it spins a thread and then beat until creamy, add cocoanut and spread between layers.

Short'nin' Bread

4 cups flour
1 cup light brown sugar
1 pound butter

Mix flour and sugar. Add butter. Place on floured surface and pat to one-half inch thickness. Cut into desired shapes and bake in moderate oven (325°-350°F.) for 20 to 25 minutes.

Brown and White Cake

‛ ½ cup butter
1½ cups sugar
4 eggs separated
2 cups pastry flour
2 teaspoons baking powder
1 teaspoon cinnamon
1 teaspoon cloves
1 teaspoon nutmeg
1 teaspoon mace
1½ tablespoons cocoa
½ cup milk

Cream butter and sugar, add egg yolks and beat well. Sift flour and baking powder and add to sugar and butter alternately with the milk. Beat the egg whites until stiff and add. Divide this mixture into two equal portions and to the one part add the spices and cocoa. Into a well-greased loaf cake pan (8x8) drop spoonfuls of each mixture. Bake in a moderate (350° F.) oven 30 minutes.

Spiced Devil's Food Cake

2 cups brown sugar
1 cup butter
2 eggs
1 cup buttermilk
3 cups flour
4 squares melted cooking chocolate
1½ tablespoons cinnamon
1 teaspoon allspice
1 teaspoon cloves
1 teaspoon baking soda dissolved in
½ cup boiling water
1 teaspoon vanilla

Cream sugar and butter and add to well beaten eggs; then add milk, chocolate, and beat flour in lightly, adding a teaspoonful of vanilla and spices. Add soda dissolved in boiling water. Bake in layer cake tins in a moderate oven (350° F.) about 30 minutes.

Pickaninny Doughnuts

2 cups brown sugar
2 eggs beaten light
4 tablespoons melted butter
1 cup sweet milk
4 cups flour
3 teaspoons baking powder
½ teaspoon cinnamon
½ teaspoon salt

Mix in the order given adding the dry ingredients sifted together and a sufficient amount of flour to make a dough just soft enough to handle. Do not mix any more than necessary as this will make your doughnuts tough. Cover the board with flour and heat the fat for frying. Roll out a little dough at a time and cut into rings with an open doughnut cutter, cutting all the doughnuts preparatory to frying. When the fat is hot enough for the dough to rise to the top quickly, start to fry the doughnuts. From 3 to 4 minutes are required to fry doughnuts.

Confederate Coffee Cake

½ cup butter
1 cup sugar
3 eggs
1½ cups flour
½ cup milk
2 teaspoons baking powder
nutmeg, cinnamon, chopped nut meats, (almonds, walnuts or pecans)

Cream sugar and butter, add milk and the unbeaten eggs and mix well. Sift the flour and baking powder and blend with the sugar and butter, adding a dash of nutmeg. Pour into well-greased loaf cake pan and sprinkle the top with nutmeg, cinnamon, nuts and granulated sugar. Dot well with butter, and bake in a moderate oven 20 minutes.

Nut Bread

½ cup sugar
1 egg
½ teaspoon salt
1 cup milk
2½ cups flour
4 teaspoons baking powder
1 cup nuts, chopped

Mix all the ingredients, put in a deep pan and let stand about 20 minutes before baking. Bake in a moderate oven (350° F.) for 40 minutes.

Pineapple Upside Down Cake

½ cup butter
1 cup brown sugar
1 medium sized can sliced pineapple
2 tablespoons whole pecans

Melt butter, in large baking pan. Spread the brown sugar evenly over the pan and arrange the slices of pineapple on the brown sugar, dropping the pecans in the open spaces. Cover this arrangement with the following cake batter.

3 eggs, separated
1 cup sugar
5 tablespoons pineapple juice
1 cup pastry flour
1 teaspoon baking powder
1 pinch salt

Beat the egg yolks until light and cream in the sugar. Add the pineapple juice and the flour which has been sifted and mix with the baking powder and salt. Fold in the stiffly-beaten egg whites and pour the batter over the pineapple, baking in a moderate (375° F.) oven for about ½ hour. Turn out up-side down and place on a cake p l a t e. This may be served w i t h unsweetened whipped cream or ice cream if desired.

Butter Icing

½ cup butter
2 cups sifted 4X sugar
    cream to moisten
    flavoring

Cream butter until soft and add sugar, blending well. Moisten with cream to the consistency desired. Any flavoring may be used.

Never Fail Icing

1 cup sugar
3 tablespoons water
2 egg whites
1 tablespoon vanilla
¼ teaspoon cream of tartar
    pinch of salt

Put all the ingredients in top of a double boiler, have water boiling in lower part. Beat with egg beater constantly for seven minutes. Remove from fire and spread on cake.

Southern Whip

½ pint of cream
    juice of ½ orange
    peel of 1 orange
½ cup sherry
⅓ cup sugar
3 egg whites

Mix the sugar and orange juice together and then pour over the whole orange peel. Use a wooden spoon and crush the peel in the juice and let stand one hour and strain. Whip the cream and add the strained orange juice. Add the wine and then fold in the stiffly beaten egg whites. Serve at once.

Mocha Icing

¼ cup butter
3 teaspoons cocoa
⅔ cup confectioner's sugar (more if needed)
1 tablespoon strong, clear coffee

Cream butter, add cocoa and sugar and moisten with coffee to the consistency desired for icing.

Orange Icing

2 egg whites, unbeaten
1½ cups sugar
5 tablespoons cold water
1½ teaspoons light corn syrup
    juice and grated rind of ½ orange

Put egg whites, sugar, water and corn syrup in upper part of double boiler. Beat with egg beater until thoroughly mixed. Place over rapidly-boiling water, beat constantly with beater and cook 7 minutes, or until frosting will stand in peaks. Remove from fire, add orange juice and rind and beat until thick enough to spread. This mixture will cover 2 nine-inch layers.

Baked Orange Fluff

4 eggs
1 cup sugar
    grated rind and juice of 1 orange

Beat egg yolks very lightly; slowly add the sugar, beating constantly. Flavor with orange juice and rind. When well mixed fold in stiffly beaten egg whites. Pour into buttered baking dish and bake in moderate oven (350° F.) for about thirty-five minutes. Serve immediately with whipped cream.

Egg Nog Sauce

2 egg whites, well beaten
2 egg yolks, well beaten
2 tablespoons whipped cream
3 tablespoons sugar
1 teaspoon rum
2 teaspoons whiskey

Beat the egg yolks until thick and lemon color. Add the whites, then sugar and beat again so that they form a meringue. Next add the rum and whiskey to above and beat into this mixture the whipped cream. Serve with hot pudding.

Brown Sugar Frosting

1 cup brown sugar
    pinch cream of tartar
½ cup water
2 egg whites, beaten stiff

Combine sugar and cream of tartar (a little vinegar may be used instead of cream of tartar, if preferred) with the water in a saucepan. Place pan over medium flame and stir mixture until sugar dissolves. Cover pan and allow syrup to boil about 4 minutes. Uncover and continue cooking until syrup will form a firm ball when tried in cold water. Remove pan from flame; when all bubbling has ceased, slowly pour syrup into a large bowl in which the egg whites have been placed, beating the mixture constantly. Continue beating for 5 or 6 minutes until of right consistency to spread.

Spanish Cream

1 pint cream (heavy)
3 eggs, separated
2 teaspoons vanilla
1 tablespoon granulated gelatin
4 tablespoons sugar

Soak gelatin in ½ cup of cream. Beat egg yolks with ½ of sugar and add the balance of cream which has been scalded. Return to double boiler and cook for 2 minutes, stirring all the time. Remove from fire and stir in the gelatin. Set aside to cool. Beat whites of eggs until stiff and gradually beat in the remaining sugar. Add vanilla and fold into the custard. Rinse mold in cold water and pour in mixture. Place in ice box for 3 hours to set. Serve with whipped cream.

When I went to see Mis' Liza Jane
She was standin' in the door,
With shoes and stockin's in her hands
And feet all over the floor.

Topsy's Nut Drop Cookies

1½ cups brown sugar
1 cup butter
3 eggs
1 tablespoon cinnamon
½ teaspoon salt
1 teaspoon baking soda, dissolved in
4 tablespoons hot water
3 cups flour
1 cup seeded raisins, chopped fine
1 cup currants, chopped fine
1 cup English walnuts, chopped fine
1 teaspoon vanilla

Beat the eggs well and add the sugar and butter which have been creamed; then add the salt, cinnamon, 2½ cups sifted flour, baking soda dissolved in the hot water. Dredge fruit and nuts with remaining flour and add to mixture. Then add vanilla and drop by spoonsful on greased cookie pan. Bake in a moderate oven (350° F.) from 10 to 12 minutes.

Plantation Sour Cream Cookies

2 cups brown sugar
1 cup rich sour cream
1 cup butter
3 teaspoons baking soda
3 eggs
1 teaspoon nutmeg
1 teaspoon vanilla
4 cups flour (or enough so that it drops from the spoon nicely)

Cream the butter and sugar and add the sour cream in which the soda has been dissolved. Beat the eggs well and add. Add the vanilla, nutmeg and then the flour. Drop from a spoon on a well-greased cookie pan and bake in a moderate oven (350° F.) until well browned, about 12 minutes.

Currant Cakes

(Old-fashioned Christmas Drop Cakes)

1 pound sugar
1 pound butter
½ pound currants (mixed with some of the flour)
6 eggs
2¼ cups flour
pinch salt
rind and juice of 1 lemon

Work butter and sugar together to smooth cream, then slowly work in the whole eggs, one at a time. Add a little of the flour, rind and juice of the lemon and salt. Work in slowly the rest of the flour and the currants. Drop by spoonfuls on large buttered pans, pressing out from the center because the cakes are better when very thin.

A good plan is to heat the pan a bit and allow the cakes to melt as much as possible before putting them in the oven to bake. Be sure to butter the pans thoroughly, otherwise the thin cakes will be difficult to remove. Bake in a moderate oven (350° F.) for 10 minutes.

Plantation Ginger Cookies

1 cup dry bread crumbs
½ cup brown sugar
⅛ teaspoon salt
1 teaspoon ginger
½ teaspoon soda
2 eggs, beaten
1 teaspoon butter, melted
1 teaspoon vanilla
¼ cup molasses

Combine dry ingredients, add beaten eggs, melted butter, vanilla and molasses. Drop from spoon about 2 inches apart onto buttered baking sheet. Bake in hot oven (400° F.) 15 to 20 minutes or until brown.

Colonial Cookies

1 cup butter
2 cups sugar
3 eggs
½ cup sour milk
1 teaspoon baking soda
1½ cups flour
1 teaspoon vanilla

Blend the butter and sugar, add the well beaten eggs. Dissolve the soda in the milk and stir in gradually with the flour. Add the vanilla. Place on floured board, roll, chill, cut with cookie cutter and bake in moderate oven (350° F.) 10 minutes.

Florida Orange Cookies

¼ cup butter
¾ cup sugar
1 egg
¼ cup orange juice
2 teaspoons baking powder
3 cups flour

Cream butter and sugar, add juice and the grated rind of one orange. Add well-beaten egg and gradually the flour to which the baking powder has been added. Place on a floured board and roll thin. Cut with cookie cutter and bake in moderate oven (350° F.) for 12 minutes.

Brownies - Chocolate Indians

⅔ cup sifted flour
½ teaspoon baking powder
¼ teaspoon salt
6½ tablespoons butter or other shortening
2 squares unsweetened chocolate, melted
1 cup sugar
2 eggs, beaten well
1 teaspoon vanilla
½ cup walnut meats, broken

Sift the flour once. After measuring, add baking powder and salt. Sift again. Then add butter to melted chocolate and blend. Cream sugar and eggs; add the chocolate mixture. Beat thoroughly. Add flour, vanilla and nuts. Bake in a greased pan, preferably 8x8x2 inches, in a moderate oven (350° F.) for 35 minutes. Before removing from the pan, cut in squares. This recipe will make two dozen brownies.

New Orleans Pralines

1½ cups sugar
½ cup cream
1 teaspoon butter
½ teaspoon vanilla
2 cups pecan meats, chopped

Boil the sugar and cream together until it forms a firm ball when tried in cold water. Add butter and vanilla; remove from fire, cool and beat until creamy. Add the broken nut meats and stir well. Drop by tablespoonfuls on buttered paper and allow to become firm.

Florida Cocoanut Pralines

2 cups sugar
2 cups freshly-grated cocoanut
½ cup water

Cook the sugar and water together until it makes a syrup. Take from fire and add the cocoanut. Cook again, stirring constantly, until it forms a soft ball when tried in cold water. Drop on buttered platter and set aside to cool and harden.

Goober Brittle

2 cups granulated sugar
1½ cups shelled peanuts, coarsely chopped
salt

Place sugar in heavy iron or agate pan and melt it over a low flame. Stir constantly so as not to allow sugar to scorch. When sugar has become a thin golden syrup, remove from flame; stir in the nuts and a few grains of salt. Spread candy on ungreased tin to harden. Mark into squares when nearly cold, or break into irregular pieces when hardened.

Candied Orange or Grapefruit Peel

3 grapefruit peelings or 6 orange peelings
1 teaspoon salt
3 cups sugar
1 cup water

Wash fruit and peel carefully, removing all of the pulp. Cut into strips about ¼ inch wide, add 1 teaspoon salt to peel and cover with water. Boil for fifteen minutes, then pour off the water and add fresh water. Boil for about twenty minutes. Change the water again and boil for another twenty minutes. After the third boiling, drain and cover with 2½ cups of sugar and 1 cup water. Boil, stirring occasionally until the syrup has boiled away. Spread on crumpled paper and before it is entirely cold roll the peel strips in the other ½ cup of sugar.

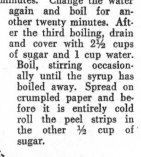

Georgia Pecan Brownies

2 egg whites
1 cup brown sugar
½ teaspoon maple flavoring
1 cup pecans, chopped
1 cup fine dry bread crumbs

Beat egg whites stiff, add sugar and flavoring. Stir well. Combine nuts and crumbs, and fold into egg whites. Shape into small balls, place on buttered baking tin, bake in slow oven until brown (325° F.).

Aunt Sarah's Fudge

2 cups sugar
2 squares unsweetened chocolate
1 cup table cream
1 tablespoon butter
1 teaspoon vanilla

Cook ingredients together without stirring until they form a soft ball when dropped in water. Cool and beat until creamy. Add chopped nuts and vanilla. Pour on a buttered dish and cut in one-inch squares when cool.

Grandmother's Caramels

3 cups brown sugar
1 cup melted butter
½ cup milk
¾ cup scraped chocolate

Combine all ingredients and cook slowly until a hard ball forms when tried in water. When done add one teaspoon vanilla and pour into greased pan. When cool, cut in squares. This candy is very apt to burn if not watched closely.

Pear Chips

4 pounds pears, sliced
3½ pounds sugar
2 lemons, sliced
½ strip crystallized ginger, chopped
4 cups water

Make a syrup of the sugar and water, add the spices and pears and boil the fruit for 1 hour. Pour into jelly glasses and seal.

Pecan Fondant

3 cups sugar
1 cup water
1½ tablespoons butter
1 teaspoon vanilla
⅛ teaspoon salt
2 cups pecan meats, chopped

Cook sugar and water until it forms a soft ball when tried in cold water. Remove from fire and beat until creamy; add the butter, vanilla, salt and nut meats and pour into a buttered dish to cover bottom ½ inch deep. When set, cut in squares.

Roll, Jordan, Roll!
Roll, Jordan, Roll!
I wants to go to Heaven when I die
To see old Jordan roll!

Cheese Appetizer For the Master's Cocktail

2 egg whites
1 cup grated cheese
¼ cup grated stale bread crumbs
dash of cayenne
Beat whites of two eggs to a very stiff froth, and add one cup of grated cheese, cayenne and ¼ cup bread crumbs. Pat into small balls and fry in deep fat.

The Delicious Appetizer

½ pound freshly-sliced dried beef
2 packages cream cheese
1½ tablespoons onion juice
2 teaspoons Worcestershire sauce
Blend the onion juice and Worcestershire sauce into the cream cheese and roll into small balls; add a bit of cream to thin the mixture if necessary. Place the cheese ball on the edge of a slice of dried beef and roll, tucking the edges in as you go. If this does not hold it can be fastened with a toothpick.

Pigs in Blankets

12 large oysters
12 slices bacon
1 pimento
½ teaspoon salt
dashes of cayenne
pinch of pepper
Season oysters with salt and pepper. Slice pimento into twelve strips, placing one piece on each oyster. Wrap each oyster with a slice of bacon, closing bacon with a toothpick or skewer. Broil for about eight minutes, browning bacon to a golden crisp.

Welsh Rarebit

3 tablespoons butter
1 pound American cheese, dry
1 teaspoon Worcestershire sauce
½ cup milk
2 eggs
½ teaspoon salt
½ teaspoon mustard
Melt the butter, add the cheese which has been cut in small pieces, and cook in a double boiler over hot water, stirring continuously, until the cheese is melted. Add the salt, mustard, Worcestershire and then pour in the milk gradually, stirring constantly. Then add the slightly-beaten eggs and stir until it becomes thick. Serve instantly on crisp toast. Beer may be substituted for milk.

Avocado Canapés

Cut small rounds of bread, and toast both sides. Spread each with the following mixture: Peel avocados and put through the ricer. Add 1 tablespoon of onion juice, 1 tablespoon lemon juice, cayenne, salt and pepper to taste. Mix with just enough mayonnaise to hold together. Press half a plain or stuffed olive on each canapé before serving.

Shrimp Avocado Cocktail

(From the Heart of the Southland)

Take an equal portion of shrimp and alligator pears (avocado), cut into small pieces and serve with a sauce made by stirring together 2 tablespoons of mayonnaise, 2 tablespoons ketchup, 1 tablespoon each of finely-chopped fresh tomatoes, finely-chopped green peppers and chili sauce.

Sherry Wine Jelly

2¾ cups boiling water
¼ cup cold water
1 cup sherry wine
juice and rind 2 lemons
2 tablespoons gelatin
1 cup sugar
2 sticks cinnamon
Add cinnamon and lemon juice and rind to boiling water and let stand over low flame until ready to use. Soak gelatin in cold water for 5 minutes. Then add gelatin to hot mixture and stir well. Add sherry wine and sugar and strain through cheesecloth. Pour into mold and place in ice box until set. Serve with whipped cream if desired.

Christening Cake

7 eggs
¾ pound butter
4 cups flour
4 cups sugar
2 heaping teaspoons baking powder
3 teaspoons nutmeg
1 cup sherry
1 cup chopped pecans
1½ pounds raisins
Cream butter and sugar together until well blended. Separate the eggs and beat yolk until light and lemon colored, then add to butter and sugar and mix thoroughly. Sift flour, baking powder and nutmeg together and add alternately with the sherry wine. Add raisins and pecan meats. Fold in the stiffly beaten egg whites and bake in a large well-buttered cake pan in slow oven (300° F.) for 4 hours.

Some Southern homes make quite an event of the "Guest Breakfast" which frequently consists of fruit, chicken hash, hot cakes, sausage, corn bread, pie and coffee ... and then there is that celebrated ritual known as the "Kentucky Breakfast" which is said to consist of a big beefsteak, a quart of bourbon and a houn dog ... the dog eats the beefsteak.

Mint Julep

Few folks agree as to what should constitute a really good mint julep. The controversy dates back to Captain Marryat who contended that he had learned how to make the real julep with fair success. Following his instructions, we do not crush the sprigs of tender mint shoots, we use a little sugar and equal portions of peach and common brandy, and we fill our glass with shaved ice. "Stalactites" of ice will form on the tumbler; and as the ice melts, we drink.

A Georgia writer of fifty years ago summed up the matter thus: "The mint julep still lives, but is by no means fashionable. Somehow the idea has gotten abroad that the mint ought to be crushed and shaken up with water and whisky in equal proportions. No man can fall in love with such a mixture."

Then there is the Kentucky colonel who advises crushing the mint within the glass until no place has been left untouched. We are then to throw away the mint; in so doing, "it is a sacrifice." This is "the one way of perfection" in concocting this "most delectable libation of man."

For each glass of mint julep, dissolve two lumps of sugar in enough water to form a sort of oily syrup. In a glass crush a few sprigs of tender mint shoots until most of the mint essence has been extracted. Remove the mint from the glass; fill the glass with cracked ice, and pour in the quantity of Bourbon desired. Allow the Bourbon to become thoroughly chilled and then add the heavy sugar syrup. Let the glass stand for a few moments, not stirring it at all. Place sprigs of fresh mint around the rim of the glass; serve immediately.

Planter's Punch
(See the World Through Rose-Colored Glasses)

Dissolve a tablespoonful of sugar in a large glass, add one wineglassful of Jamaica rum, one-half wineglassful of good brandy. Squeeze into this the juice of one-half lemon and a little pineapple juice. Pour into tall glass and then fill glass with shaved ice and mix thoroughly with a spoon. The glass should be frosted when the drink is served.

North Carolina Syllabub
(A Builder-Upper)

1 pint cream, a day old
½ cup fresh milk
½ cup sweet cider
½ teaspoon vanilla
½ cup sugar
   a little nutmeg

Chill the ingredients and make shortly before you are ready to serve. Mix all of the ingredients in a mixing bowl except the cream, which should be beaten lightly. Add cream and beat again. Sprinkle a little nutmeg on top and serve. Whiskey or brandy may be used instead of cider. A tablespoon of sherry may be added if desired.

Egg Nog
(Individual Portion)

1 egg
2 teaspoons sugar
   cold milk
   dash vanilla
   nutmeg, grated
2 tablespoons cream
1 whisky glass Brandy, Rye or Bourbon

Separate egg. Beat yolk until very light with sugar, add white, beaten stiff. Add 2 tablespoons sweet cream, brandy or whiskey, vanilla; fill glass with cold milk. Grate the nutmeg on top.

Spiced Cider

1 quart sweet cider
¼ cup sugar
8 short pieces of stick cinnamon
12 whole cloves
8 whole allspice
   pinch salt

Mix all of the ingredients in a pot and heat to a boiling point. Let stand for several hours. Reheat, remove the whole spices and serve hot with cookies or cake.

Zazarac Cocktail
(One Portion)

⅓ pony Bacardi rum
⅓ pony rye whiskey
1/6 pony anisette
1/6 pony gum
1 dash angostura bitters
1 dash orange bitters
3 dashes absinthe

Put all the ingredients in a cocktail shaker with some ice. Shake well, strain, pour in glass and serve.

Orange Julep

1 quart orange juice
1 cup sugar
6 limes (juice)
½ cup minced mint
1 pint charged water
   ice

Mix orange juice, sugar, lime juice and minced mint. Place on ice one hour. Half fill glasses with ice, add prepared juice and sprigs of mint.

Tom and Jerry Southern Style

Beware! A sudden jolt of this has been known to stop a victim's watch, snap both of his suspenders and crack his glass eye right across . . . all in the same motion.—COBB.

Beat 12 eggs very well and slowly add 1 pound of 4X sugar, continuing to beat. For each serving pour one large jigger of whiskey into a cup. Fill each cup ⅔ full of boiling water; put spoonful of egg mixture on top and a dash of nutmeg and serve. WOW-W!

Idle Hour Cocktail

⅔ gin
1/6 Italian vermouth
1/6 grapefruit juice

Mix all the ingredients, stir well, but do not shake.

CPSIA information can be obtained at www.ICGtesting.com
Printed in the USA
BVOW08s1913250615

406233BV00001B/24/P